TREATISE ON GROUPS OF ELEMENTS

TREATISE ON GROUPS OF ELEMENTS

THE ABHIDHARMA-DHĀTUKĀYA-PĀDAŚĀSTRA

English Translation of Hsüan-tsang's
Chinese Version Edited with Critical Notes

SWATI GANGULY

EASTERN BOOK LINKERS

DELHI : : INDIA

Publishers :
EASTERN BOOK LINKERS
5825, New Chandrawal, Jawahar Nagar,
Delhi-110007 Ph.: 2520287

First Edition : 1994

ISBN : 81-86339-06-X

Lasertypesetting & Printing at :
AMAR PRINTING PRESS
Phone : 7252362

Dedicated to

My Beloved Mother

Mrs. ANIMA MUKHERJI

CONTENTS

PREFACE

The seven Buddhist texts of the *Sarvāstivāda Abhidharma* tradition are preserved mainly in their Chinese translations. Only a few studies on this extensive literature have been done so far. Among the texts the *Abhidharma-Dhātukāya-pādaśāstra* represents the transitional phase of Buddhist analytical philosophy manifested in the evolution of the *Sarvāstivāda Abhidharma* in Northwestern India. The original Sanskrit versions of the texts, unfortunately lost at present, was procured by Hsüan-tsang, the great monk scholar of China, during his visit to India. Later the text was translated into Chinese.

Our study seeks to present a critical English translation of the Chinese version of the text available in *Taisho* 1540. Composed in classical Chinese, the text contains a large number of *Ābhidhārmic* terms with their definitions and elaborations. For a clear understanding of the text, a comparative analysis of those terms has been made in the notes to the Chapters.

The study aims at a broader understanding of rare early Sanskrit sources on Buddhist psychology with reference to mental faculties as detailed in the text., The *Ābhidhārmic* scheme of the text provided a firm basis for the later *Sarvāstivāda Abhidharma* tradition in India, China and Japan. From this viewpoint, the study of the text may also be helpful for a deeper knowledge of the formation of the *Abhidharma* in the process of systematization of the Buddhist doctrines in general and of the development of the *Sarvāstivāda* in particular. The study seeks not only to fulfill some serious research gaps in the area, but also to make a systematic reconstruction of the various aspects of the early Buddhist philosophy from Buddhist textual references in Pāli, Sanskrit and classical Chinese.

I am thankful to the University Grants Commission for financial support to the research, field work, and completion of writing of the present study during 1988-93 while I was working as a Research Scientist in the Department of Buddhist Studies, University of Delhi. For advice and ideas on this project I am indebted to Prof. Mahesh Tiwary and Prof. K.K. Mittal. I would like to thank Prof. Huang Xin Chuang, Director, Institute of Asia - Pacific Studies, Beijing, China, and Prof. Whalen Lai, Chairman, Deptt. of Religious Studies, University of California, Davis, USA, for useful suggestions on the work. Thanks are due here to Prof. Sanghasena Singh, friends, and colleagues in the Deptt. of Buddhist Studies for their support and encouragement without which this project would not have been possible. For use of rare materials must specially thank Delhi University Library, Asiatic Society Library and Sanskrit College Library in Calcutta. Finally I thank my husband Dr. Shivaji Ganguly and my daughter Arundhati for encouraging all my efforts.

Delhi, March, 1994 **SWATI GANGULY**

ABBREVIATIONS

AA	:	*Abhidharmāmṛta*
ADPS	:	*Abhidharmadhātukāyapādaśāstra*
AK	:	*Abhidharmakośa*
AKB	:	*Abhidharmakośabhāṣya*
AN	:	*Aṅguttaranikāya*
AKV	:	*Abhidharmakośavyākhyā*
ATTH	:	*Aṭṭhaśālinī*
CWSL	:	*Ch'eng-wei-shih-lun*
DHS	:	*Dhammasaṅgaṇi*
DN	:	*Dīghanikāya*
MN	:	*Majjhimanikāya*
MV	:	*Mahāvyutpatti*
PP	:	*Puggalapaññatti*
PTS	:	Pali Text Society
SN	:	*Saṃyuttanikāya*
TI	:	*Taishō shinshu daizōkyo*
VIBH	:	*Vibhaṅga*
VMS	:	*Vijñaptimātratāsiddhi*

INTRODUCTION

THE TEXT

The Sanskrit original of the *Abhidharma - Dhātukāya- Pādaśāstra* (hereafter *ADPS*) belonging to the *Sarvāstivāda* school of Buddhism has not yet been found. Fortunately however, the text is preserved in its Chinese version (title *A-p'i-ta-mo-chieh-shen-tsu-lun*) by Hsüan-tsang (599- 664), the great Chinese Buddhist monk, who procured the original probably during his journey through India. The systematic exposition of the mental attributes *(dhātu)* and their mutual relations in the text provides a rare insight for the reconstruction of the transitional phases of the Buddhist analytical philosophy and psychology.

The *ADPS*, popularly known as the *Dhātukāya* is included among the seven basic *Abhidharma* texts, i.e., the *Jñānaprasthāna* and the six supplementary texts - the *Saṅgītiparyāya,* the *Prakaraṇapāda,* the *Vijñānakāya,* the *Dhātukāya,* the *Dharmaskandha,* and the *Prajñaptiśāstra.* These were composed by *Sarvāstivādin* scholar monks in Sanskrit language. So far as the *ADPS* is concerned, at the end of its three main divisions *(chüans),* the text is mentioned as belonging to the *Sarvāstivāda* school. All the seven texts were widely studied in Kashmir from where those were transported outside India, specially to China. Unfortunately the originals which existed in more than one versions, are all lost in India. Preserved in Chinese and Japanese, the text along with the other six *Abhidharma* texts, were highly esteemed by the followers of *Chü-she* school in China and *Kusha* school in Japan.

The existence of the original text entitled '*Dhātukāya*' is proved by the fact that although the Sanskrit originals of the seven texts do not exist, the Sanskrit titles of the texts and the names of the authors of the texts are available in Yaśomitra's *Sphutārthā* on the *AK* I.3 which mentions that Pūrṇa is the composer of the *Dhātukāya*. Bu-ston, the famous Tibetan writer of the fourteenth century also mentions the same Sanskrit titles of the seven *Abhidharma* texts along with their Tibetan titles. Modern studies have proved that the Sanskrit titles of the seven *Abhidharma* texts agree with corresponding Tibetan works, although those works excepting the *Prajñaptiśāstra* do not exist in the *Kanjur* or *Tanjur*.

That the Chinese text of the *ADPS* belong to the Seven texts of *Sarvāstivāda Abhidharma* tradition is also confirmed from Chinese sources. Fu-kuang, a disciple of Hsüan-tsang, mentions the Chinese name of the *Dhātukāya* among the six supplementary texts of *Abhidharma*. The Chinese name of the *Dhātukāya* also appears in a colophon by K'uei-chi, another disciple of Hsüan-tsang as one of the six *pāda* works to the *Jñānaprasthāna* which belongs to the *Sarvāstivāda* school (Takakusu : 1905 : 79).

The Sanskrit form of the title of the *ADPS* is taken from '*Chi- yüan-lu*', a catalogue of the Sacred texts in the '*Chi-yüan*' period (1264-94). It is said that the Chinese titles of all the Chinese Buddhist texts were restored to their Sanskrit forms along with the Chinese transliterations in this catalogue after a detailed comparison of the Chinese Buddhist texts with the Tibetan *Kanjur*. This catalogue helped a great deal the modern scholars to identify the Sanskrit works with the Chinese (details in *ibid,* 81).

No commentary on the *ADPS* is available. However, a Chinese colophon provides important informations regarding the text. A colophon by K'uei-chi (died A.D. 682, Chinese text in T. 1540, Vol.26) reads : "the

Dhātukāya is one of the six *pādas* on the *Jñānaprasthāna*, which belongs to the *Sarvāstivāda* school. My personal master, Hiuen- tsang, finished a Chinese translation of this text on the 4th day of the 6th moon in the 3rd year of the *Hung-tse* period of the Augustan dynasty (i.e., A.D. 663) while staying at the *Yu-hua* palace. The larger text of this treatise consisted of 6,000 *ślokas*. Afterwards, as it was found too complicated, it was abridged by a scholar in two forms, one in 900 *ślokas,* the other in 500 *ślokas*. The present translation consists of 830 *ślokas*. The original text was composed by the Venerable Shi-yu (Vasumitra)..." (See Takakusu, *ibid,* p. 111.).

Hsüan-tsang (Travels:) claims that Vasumitra composed the *ADPS* near Puṣkarāvatī in the Gandhara. However, according to Yaśomitra *(Sphutārthā, AK.* I.3) and Bu-ston, Pūrṇa was the author of the *Dhātukāya.*

The text under discussion has been retranslated only in Japanese language (Nakamura: 1980: 106). Synoptic analysis of the text is available in Takaskusu : 1905; Watanabe: 1980; Encylopaedia of Buddhism: 1989; Swati Ganguly : 1992 etc. Brief discussions or passing references on the texts are available in A. Banerjee : 1979; N. Dutt: 1978; 1925; Poussin: 1971; Nanjio : 1883 etc.

TITLE OF THE ADPS

In the title *Abhidharma* - Dhātukāyapādaśāstra, the word *dhātu* (element) refers to all mental faculties or attributes which are considered as separate elements in the *Abhidharma* tradition, '*Dhātu*' is derived from the root "*Dhar*" which means " to hold, to bear". Thus "that which carries its own characteristic mark is *dhātu*". They are so called since they are devoid of being or life *(nissatta-nijjīva)*. The word "*kāya*" means " body" or "group".

Thus *Dhātukāya* means groups of attributes which constitute mind itself. Chapter I of the *ADPS* is devoted to the enumerations and definitions of the mental attributes. Chapter II deals with the association and dissociation, inclusion and exclusion of the above attributes which are again grouped into the three categories of 18 elements, 12 bases and 5 aggregates. Those attributes are explained in Pāli *Abhidhamma* texts like the *Dhammasaṅgaṇi, the Vibhaṅga* and the *Dhātukathā,* and in the early Sanskrit *Abhidharma* texts like the *Jñānaprasthāna,* the *Prakaraṇapāda* and the *Vijñānakāyapāda.* However, the *dhātus* are exclusively treated only in the *ADPS.* Although the *ADPS* has some striking similarities with the *Dhātukathā* in the treatment of the classification of the mental states, yet the details of the characteristics of the functions of the states are not detailed in the manner of the first chapter of the *ADPS.* Thus the *ADPS* is the only *Abhidharmic* text that provides systematic and complete informations about the mental attributes or *dhātus* which are known as *cetasikas* in *Pāli Abhidhamma.*

CONTENT ANALYSIS OF THE ADPS

The mental attributes or the *cetasikas* are systematically discussed in the *ADPS.* In the first Chapter the 'partitive' functions of the mind are classified in the enumeration of subjects:

Ten Basic states, *mahābhūmikadharma*

Ten Impure states, *kleśamahābhūmikadharma*

Ten Minor Impure states, *upakleśamahābhūmikadharma*

Five Moral impurities, *kleśa*

Five Views, *dṛṣṭi*

Five Contacts, *sparśa*

Five Faculties *indriya*

Five *dharmas*

Six Groups of Knowledge *vijñānakāya*

Six Groups of Contact *sparśakāya*

Six Groups of Feeling *vedanākāya*

Six Groups of Notion *saṃjñākāya*

Six Groups of Volition *cetanākāya*

Six Groups of Craving *tṛṣṇākāya*

The classification of the thirty Mind-states in the *Abhidharma* appears for the first time in the *ADPS.*

After the enumeration of subjects, the *ADPS* defines the items in the list (see *translation,* pp. 14-30). The definitions are done in early *Ābhidhārmic* style, seen also in the Pāli *Abhidhamma* texts of the *Dhammasaṅgaṇi* and the *Vibhaṅga.* They consist of synonymous terms to clarify the concepts regarding particular terms. This was done probably to safeguard the doctrines from sectarian innovations. Again regarding sensations, in all the definitions, the typical *Ābhidharmic* time-reference like " has seen, sees, will or may see" is always there.

In the second Chapter of the *ADPS,* the mutual relations of the 88 mental categories are discussed. The mental categories are treated under the three categories of elements, bases and aggregates. In each of the 16 sections a mental state of inquiry is paired with the category next in order. In the first three sections the states of inquiry are examined with reference to the nature and mutual relations of the mental states in terms of association *(saṃprayukta)* and dissociation *(viprayukta).* The co-existence of the mind states and their attributes are considered as *saṃprayoga.* The detachment of the mind-states from the attributes are considered as *viprayoga.*

Sections 4-16 in the second chapter examine the mutual relations of the mental categories associated with and dissociated from the state of inquiry in terms of inclusion *(saṃgṛhīta)* and noh-inclusion *(asaṃgrhīta)* in respect of both the mental and the material elements. The members of elements, bases and aggregates under which a state of inquiry is included is given and the remaining numbers of the elements, bases, and aggregates are those which are not included. This method of exposition provides systematic and complete information about the mental categories from one particular aspect.

The method of inquiry in mutual relation is the following:-

Feeling etc. are mental attributes in terms of

1. Inclusion and non-inclusion of a particular *dhātu* with reference to 18 *dhātus,* 12 *āyatanas* and 5 *skandhas.* Thus questions are raised to show how a particular *dharma* is included and not included in so many *āyatanas, dhātus,* and *skandhas.* In this way, the identity, difference and resemblance of the mental attributes under consideration become clear. The principle of inclusion and non-inclusion, however, is used in respect of both mental and material *dharmas.*

2. The interrelations of the three categories in terms of association suggests the " consideration of concurrence and coexistence of mental actions." The mental categories having common characteristics are associated together. These are the four characteristics:

1. The arising together

2. Ceasing to function together

3. Having the common object

4. Having the common base

The categories which do not possess these characteristics, are said to be " dissoicated".

For example, in Section 4 of the *ADPS*, the interrelation of mental categories is examined in terms of association and dissociation of those categories, which are associated and dissociated from those which are associated and dissociated from the categories of inquiry. It also shows the inclusion and non-inclusion of those categories. The purpose of this method is to provide systematic and complete information about the ultimate realities from different standpoints.

From historical viewpoint, the classification of contents like *rūpa, citta, cetasika, asaṃkhāta* (asaṃskṛta) etc., and a detailed study on those classifications may be regarded as the characteristics of the middle period of the *Abhidharma.* The *ADPS,* dealing mainly with different states of mind and their mutual relations, may belong to the latter period. Also, the method of *Ābhidhārmic* study adopted in the *ADPS* in Chapter II regarding the " consideration of the subject- matter from the point of view of connotation and denotation" *(saṃgraha)*, and the "consideration of the concurrence and co-existence of mental action" *(saṃprayoga)*, reveals the *Ābhidharmic* characteristics of the middle period (details in Encyclopedia: I, 47). However the study of the contents of the *ADPS* unveils the features of *Ābhidhārmic* tradition which are considerably different from the Pāli *Ābhidhāmmic* tradition. The latter is believed to be the preserver of the earliest record of the *Abhidharma.* From a comparative study of the method of the exposition of the mental categories and of the arrangement of the topics in the text of the *ADPS* and the early texts of Pāli *Abhidhamma,* i.e., the *Dhammasaṅgaṇi* the *Vibhaṅga,* and the *Dhātukathā,* we may assume that those texts were compiled at about the same stage of the development of the *Abhidharma.*

TRANSLATION

A-P'I-TA-MO-CHIEH-SHEN-TSU-LUN

TREATISE ON GROUPS OF ELEMENTS

ABHIDHARMA-DHĀTUKĀYAPĀDAŚĀSTRA

CHAPTER I

CHIEF SUBJECTS

1. ENUMERATION OF MAIN SUBJECTS

1.0 The main subjects of the *ADPS* are:-

(i) Three Mind-states (*bhūmi*)[1] each of ten varieties[2]

(ii) Five Moral Impurities (*kleśa*)

(iii) Five Views (*dṛṣṭi*)

(iv) Five Contacts (*sparśa*)

(v) Five Faculties (*indriya*)

(vi) Five *Dharmas*

(vii) Thirty-six Groups (*kāya*) resulting from the six organs of sense

1.1. There are ten *dharmas* having Basic states (*mahāhūmika*), ten *dharmas* having Impure states (*kleśamahābhūmika*), ten *dharmas* having Minor Impure states (*parīttakleśabhūmika*), five Moral Impurities, five Views, five Contacts, five Faculties, Five *Dharmas,* six Groups of Consciousness (*vijñānakāya*), six Groups of volition (*cetanākāya*), six Groups of Craving (*tṛṣṇākāya*).

1.2 What are the ten *dharmas* having Basic states?[3] They are - (i) Feeling (*vedanā*), (ii) Notion (*saṃjñā*), (iii) Volition (*cetanā*), (iv) Contact (*sparśa*), (v) Attention (*manaskāra*), (vi) Desire (*chanda*), (vii) Approbation (*adhimokṣa*), (viii) Memory (*smṛti*), (ix) Concentration (*samādhi*) and (x) Discernment (*prajñā*).[4]

1.3 What are then ten *dharmas* having Impure states?[5] They are- (i) Unbelief (*āśraddhya*), (ii) Idleness (*kauśīdya*), (iii) Forgetfulness (*muṣitāsmṛti*), (iv) Distraction *(vikṣepa)*, (v) Ignorance *(avidyā)*, (vi) Non-discernment *(asamprajanya)*, (vii) Wrong Attention *(ayoniśomanaskāra)*, (viii) False Resolve *(mithyādhimokṣa)*, (ix) Restlessness *(auddhatya)* and (x) Carelessens *(pramāda)*.[6]

1.4 What are the ten *dharmas* having Minor Impure states.?[7] They are- (i) Fury *(krodha)*, (ii) Enmity *(upanāha)*, (iii) Hypocrisy *(mrakṣa)*, (iv) Vexation *(pradāśa)*, (v) Envy *(īrṣyā)*, (vi) Parsimony *(mātsarya)*, (vii) Deception *(śāṭhya)*, (viii) Duplicity *(māyā)*, (ix) Pride *(mada)* and (x) Harmfulness *(vihiṃsā)*.[8]

1.5 What are the five Moral Impurities ?[9] They are- (i) Sensuous Attachment *(kāmarāga)*, (ii) Attachment for Material existence *(rūparāga)*, (iii) Attachment for Immaterial existence *(arūparāga)*, (iv) Hatred *(dveṣa)*, and (v) Doubt *(vicikitsā)*.

1.6 What are the five Views ?[10] They are - (i) Personality belief *(satkāyadṛṣṭi)*., (ii) Viewpoint of nihilism or eternalism *(antagrāhadṛṣṭi)*. *(iii)* Wrong View *(mithyādṛṣṭi)*. (iv) Wrong View as in attachment to a particular opinion *(dṛṣṭiparāmarśa)* and (vi) Wrong View as in attachment to mere rules and rituals *(śīlavrataparāmarśa)*[11].

1.7 What are called the five Contacts?[12] They are (i) Contact by sensorial reaction *(pratighasparśa)*, (ii) Verbal or Mental Contact *(adhivacanasparśa)*, (iii) Contact by knowledge *(vidyāsparśa)*, (iv) Contact by ignorance *(avidyāsparśa)*, and (v) Contact by neither-knowledge-nor-non-knowledge (*na-vidyā-nāvidyā-sparśa*).

1.8 What are the five Faculties?[13] They are—(i) Faculty for feeling pleasure *(sukhendriya)*, (ii) Faculty for feeling pain *(duḥkhendriya)*, (iii) Faculty for feeling satisfaction *(saurmanasyendriya)*, (iv) Faculty for feeling dissatisfaction *(daurmanasyendriya)*, and (v) Faculty for feeling indifference *(upekṣendriya)*.

1.9 What are the five *Dharmas*?[14] They are- (i) Searching state of mind *(vitarka)*, (ii) Investigation *(vicāra)*, (iii) Consciousness *(vijñāna)*, (iv) Absence of sense of shame *(āhrīkya)*, and (v) Absence of fear of blame *(anapatrāpya)*.

1.10 What are the six Groups of Consciousness?[15] They are (i) Eye-Consciousness *(cakṣurvijñāna)*, (ii) Ear-Consciousness *(śrotravijñāna)*, (iii) Olfactory Consciousness *(ghrāṇavijñāna)*, (iv) Gustatory Consciousness *(jihvāvijñāna)*, (v) Body-Consciousness *(kāyavijñāna)*, and (vi) Mind-Consciousness *(manovijñāna)*.

1.11 What are the six Groups of Contact?[16] They are- (i) Visual Contact *(cakṣusparśa)*, (ii) Contact by hearing *(śrotrasparśa)*, (iii) Contact by smelling *(ghraṇasparśa)*, (iv) Contact by tasting *(jihvāsparśa)*, (v) Tactile Contact *(kāyavijñāna)*, and (vi) Mental Contact *(manasparśa)*.

1.12 What are the six Groups of Feeling?[17] They are (i) Feeling that is born of contact with the organ of view along with its object *(cakśusaṃsparśajā vedanā)*, (ii) Feeling that is born of contact with the organ of hearing along with its object *(śrotrasaṃsparśajā vedanā)*. (iii) Feeling that is born of contact with the organ of smelling along with its object *(ghrāṇasaṃsparśajā vedanā)*, (iv) Feeling that is born of contact with the organ of tasting along with its object *(jihvāsaṃsparśajā vedanā)*, (v) Feeling that is born of contact with the body along with its objects *(kāyasaṃsparśajā vedanā)*, and (vi) Feeling that is born of contact with the mind along with its object *(manaḥsaṃsparśajā vedanā)*.

1.13 What are the six Groups of Notion?[18] They are (i) Notion born of contact with eye *(cakṣusaṃsparśajā saṃjñā)*, (ii) Notion born of contact with ear *(śrotrasaṃsparśajā saṃjñā)*, (iii) Notion born of contact with nose *(ghrāṇasaṃsparśajā samjñā)*, (iv) Notion born of contact with tongue *(jihvāsaṃsparśajā saṃjñā)* Notion born of contact with body, and (vi) Notion born of contact with mind *(manaḥsaṃsparśajā saṃjñā)*.

1.14. What are the six Groups of Volition?[19] They are (i) Volition born of visual contact *(cakṣusaṃsparśajā cetanā)*, (ii) Volition born of contact with ear *(śrotrasaṃsparśajā cetanā)*, (iii) Volition born of contact with nose *(ghrāṇasaṃsparśajā cetanā)*, (iv) Volition born of contact with tongue *(jihvāsaṃsparśajā cetanā)*, (v) Volition born of contact with body *(kāyasamṣparśajā cetanā)*, and (vi) Volition born of contact with mind *(manaḥsaṃsparśajā cetanā)*

1.15 What are the six Groups of Craving?[20] They are (i) Craving born of visual contact *(cakṣusaṃsparśajā tṛṣṇā)*, (ii) Craving born of contact with ear *(śrotrasaṃsparśajā tṛṣṇā)*, (iii) Craving born of contact with nose *(ghrāṇasaṃsparśajā tṛṣṇā)* (iv) Craving born of contact with tongue (*Jiḥvasaṃsparśajā vedanā*), (v) Craving born of contact with body (*kāyasaṃsparsājā vedanā*), and (vi) Craving born of contact with mind *(manaḥsaṃsparśajā tṛṣṇā)*.

2. THREE MIND-STATES

(i) Ten Basic states

2.1.1. What is Feeling? That which is feeling, similar to feeling, every similar feeling, feeling in present, past and future. This is called Feeling.[21]

2.1.2. What is Notion? That which is notion, similar to notion, notion in present, past and future. This is called Notion.[22]

2.1.3. What is Volition? That which is volition, similar to volition, volition in present, past and future. This is called Volition.[23]

2.1.4. What is Contact? That which is contact, similar to contact, contact in present, past and future. This is called Contact.[24]

2.1.5. What is Attention? That which is mind's reaction to respective object, the similar, attention in present, past and future. This is called Attention.[25]

2.1.6. What is Desire? That which is desire, desirable, the state of desire, desiring, pleasure, state of happiness for all, desirability, state of searching happiness, desire for action by the doer. This is called Desire.[26]

2.1.7. What is Approbation? That which is state of approbation, approbation in past and future. This is called Approbation.[27]

2.1.8. What is Memory ? That which is remembrance, recollection, remembering others, to remember, the state of not forgetting, the state of indelibility by means of the negation of the loss of the impression of the objects. The articulation of the mind, the recollection (of the appreciated object) is called Memory.[28]

2.1.9. What is Concentration ? That which is stability of mind, fairness, going steady, non-distraction, imperturbability, holding firmly, tranquility, one-pointedness of mind. This is called Concentration.[29]

2.1.10 What is Discernment ? That which is discernment of the *dharmas,* analysis of the *dharmas,* discrimination of *dharmas,* near discrimination, similar discrimination.[30]

(ii) Ten Impure states

2.2.1. What is Unbelief ? That which is the state of unbelief, not having belief, not having belief in present, not putting trust in, not permitting the practices, not submitting to belief in the past, future and present, that which makes mind impure. This is called Unbelief.[31]

2.2.2. What is Indolence ? That which is lack of zeal, not having zeal, suppressing zeal, obstruction to zeal, straightly puts a stop to zeal, does not encourage mind in present, past and future. This is called Indolence.[32]

2.2.3. What is Forgetfulness ? That which is lack of memory, wrong memory, forgetting, mind not clearly remembering, This is called Forgetfulness.[33]

2.2.4. What is Distraction ? That which is distraction of mind, state of mind having different thoughts (simultaneously), delusion of mind, state of mind not having a single object, state of mind not fixing in a single object. This is called Distraction.[34]

2.2.5. What is Ignorance ? This is ignorance of the three worlds.[35]

2.2.6. What is Non-discernment ? This is lack of comprehension with regard to discernment.[36]

2.2.7. What is Wrong Attention ? It is defiled attention.[37]

2.2.8. What is False Resolve ? That which is defiled attention associated with mental resolve, persistence of mental impression. This is called False Resolve.[38]

2.2.9. What is Restlessness? That which is the state of mind not peaceful and tranquil,[39] absolutely not peaceful and tranquil, vociferation-excitement, similarly vociferation-excitement, mind with vociferation-excitement. This is called Restlessness.[40]

2.2.10. What is Carelessness ? With regard to the abandonment of bad *dharmas*[41] and collection of good *dharmas*.[42] that which is the state of not being firm to act on, not constantly working on, not being intimate to, not putting practice in, not cultivating on, is called Carelessness.

(iii) Minor Impure states

2.3.1. What is Fury?[43] That which is fury, that which is similar, throughout fury, extreme fury, fury in past, present and future. This is called Fury.

2.3.2. What is Enmity? That which is enduring enmity of mind;[44] that which is similar, throughout enmity; constant hostility of mind. This is called Enmity.

2.3.3. What is Hypocrisy ? Hiding one's offense is called Hypocrisy.[45]

2.3.4. What is Vexation ? That which is very angry state of mind, which provokes one to utter evil words and to bite, the state of mind in a rage. This is called Vexation.[46]

2.3.5. What is Envy? That which is state of being intolerable to stand the glory of other.[47]

2.3.6. What is Parsimony ? That which is mind's attachment to wealth and *dharma* and lacking (desire) to give them away is called Parsimony.[48]

2.3.7. What is Deception ? That which is deceiving and misleading others is called Deception.[49]

2.3.8. What is Duplicity ? It is deceitful mind.[50]

2.3.9. What is Pride ? When one is devoted to one's activities of excellence with regard to beauty, wealth, talent, skill, lineage, strength and virtuousness, a great pleasure appears in oneself. This produces the state of proud exaltation; intoxicated state; a state of disturbance; disturbed mind; being proudly exalted. This is called Pride.[51]

2.3.10 What is Harmfulness? That which is the state of hurting the happiness of sentient beings and the infliction of injury and distress to them.[52]

3. FIVE MORAL IMPURITIES

3.1. What is Sensuous Attachment ? With regard to greed produced from desire, that which is similar, lust, clinging, concealing, guarding, fondness, excessive pleasure. This is called Sensuous Attachment.[53]

3.2. What is Attachment for Material existence ? With regard to greed produced from material existence, that which is similar, lust, clinging, concealing, guarding, fondness, excessive pleasure. This is called Attachment for Material existence.[54]

3.3. What is Attachment for Immaterial existence ? With regard to greed produced from immaterial existence, that which is similar, lust, clinging, concealing, guarding, fondness, excessive pleasure. This is called Attachment for Immaterial existence.

3.4 What is Hatred ? That which is desire that compels one to harm the sentient beings, inwardly growing extreme hatred and anger, throughout hatred and anger, that which is similar, extreme hatred that means excessive anger, hatred and anger in present, past and future. This is called Hatred.[55]

3.5 What is Doubt ? That which is uncertainty of mind with regard to all verities.[56]

4. FIVE VIEWS

4.1. What is Personality View ? With regard to the five groups of Clinging, that which is the clinging to the 'I and mine', from which arises volition, pleasure and discrimination. This is called Personality view.[57]

4.2. What is Viewpoint of nihilism or eternalism ? With regard to the five groups of Clinging, that which is the clinging to destructibility or eternality from which arises volition, pleasure and discrimination. This is called Viewpoint of nihilism or eternalism.[58]

4.3. What is Wrong View ? With regard to the five groups of Clinging, that which is the clinging to the rejection of cause, or rejection of fruit, or rejection of action and utility, or distortion of facts from which arises volition, pleasure and discrimination. This is called Wrong View.[59]

4.4. What is Wrong View as in attachment to a particular opinion ? With regard to the five groups of Clinging, that which is clinging to a particular opinion as the ultimate, as the excellent, as the most wonderful, from which arises volition, pleasure and discrimination. This is called Wrong View as in attachment to a particular opinion.[60]

4.5. What is Wrong View as in attachment to mere rules and rituals? With regard to the five groups of Clinging, that which is the clinging to rules and rituals, takes them as purification, as conviction, or as "going beyond" from which arises volition, pleasure and discrimination. This is called Wrong View as in attachment to mere rules and rituals.[61]

5. FIVE CONTACTS

5.1. What is Contact by sensorial reaction ? That which is contact associated with fivefold cognition.[62]

5.2. What is Verbal or Mental Contact ? That which is contact associated with mind-consciousness.[63]

5.3. What is Contact by knowledge ? That which is contact without contamination.[64]

5.4. What is Contact by Ignorance ? That which is Contact with defilement.[65]

5.5. What is Contact by neither-knowledge-nor-non-knowledge ? That which is contact with neither-contamination-nor-non- defilement.[66]

6. FIVE FACULTIES[67]

6.1. What is Faculty for feeling pleasure ? That which is for feeling of pleasure born of contact; easeful pleasant experience born of bodily contact; This is called Faculty for feeling pleasure.[68]

6.2. What is Faculty for feeling pain ? That which is for unpleasant feeling born of contact; painful uneasy experience born of bodily contact. This is called Faculty of pain.[69]

6.3. What is Faculty for feeling satisfaction ? That which is for feeling satisfaction born of contact; easeful pleasant experience born of mental contact. This is called Faculty for feeling satisfaction.[70]

6.4. What is Faculty for feeling dissatisfaction ? That which is for feeling dissatisfaction born of contact; uneasy painful experience born of mental contact. This is called Faculty for feeling dissatisfaction.[71]

6.5. What is Faculty for feeling indifference ? That which is for feeling neither pain nor pleasure born of contact; neither easy nor uneasy experience born of bodily and mental contact. This is called Faculty for feeling indifference.[72]

7. FIVE DHARMAS

7.1. What is Searching state of mind? That which is (with regard to the object of mental discourse) a state of search, indication, earnest indication, past and present indication, thorough search, thorough consideration, thorough implication, discrimination, similar to that, the state of discrimination. This is called Searching state of mind.[73]

7.2. What is Investigation ? That which is (with regard to the object of mental discourse) a state of careful investigation, thorough careful investigation, making thorough careful investigation, examination, thorough examination; that which is of the nature of arising, flowing and assembling of those. This is called Investigation.[74]

7.3. What is Consciousness ? That which is the six body of cognitions starting from eye-consciousness up to mental congnition.

7.4. What is Absence of sense of shame ? That which is shamelessness, shameless, other shamelessness, sense of shamelessness, without sense of shamelessness, other sense of shamelessness, disregard, having disregard, other disregard, uneasiness, uneasy, other uneasiness, fearless, uneasiness arising from fearlessness. This is called Absence of sense of shame.[75]

7.5. What is Absence of fear of blame ? That which is not having sense of fear of blame, other absence of fear of blame, not having sense of shame, other absence of sense of shame, not having shame at one's sins, not having fear of blame at one's sins, not seeing shame and fear at one's sins. This is called Absence of fear of blame.[76]

8. SIX GROUPS OF CONSCIOUSNESS

8.1. What is Eye-consciousness ? That which is eye-consciousness born of eye and material existence; eye being the support and material existence being a condition; that which is experience with regard to eye, its consciousness and material existence. This is called Eye-consciousness.[77]

8.2. What is Ear-consciousness, Olfactory consciousness, Gustatory consciousness, Body-consciousness and Mind-consciousness ?

That which is ear-consciousness born of ear and sound, ear being the support and sound being the condition; that which is experience with regard to ear, its consciousness and sound. This is called Ear-consciousness.[78]

That which is Olfactory consciousness born of nose and smell, nose being the support and smell being the condition; that which is experience with regard to nose, its consciousness and smell. This is called Olfactory consciousness.[79]

That which is Gustatory consciousness born of tongue and taste, tongue being the support and taste being the condition; that which is experience with regard to tongue, its consciousness and taste. This is called Gustatory consciousness.[80]

That which is body-consciousness born of body and touch, body being the support and touch being the condition; that which is experience with regard to body, its consciousness and touch. This is called Body-consciousness.[81]

That which is born of mind and object, mind being the support and object being the condition; that which is experience with regard to mind, its consciousness and object. This is called Mind-consciousness.[82]

9. SIX GROUPS OF CONTACT

9.1. What is Visual contact ? That which is contact due to tripartite conjunction of eye, material existence and eye- consciousness, the last arising from the first two among which eye is the support and material existence is the condition; that which is contact in relation to eye, eye-consciousness and material existence, similar to that, the contact in present, past and future. This is called Visual contact.[83]

9.2. What is Contact by hearing, Contact by smelling, Contact by tasting, Tactile contact, and Mental contact?

Contact by hearing is that which is contact due to tripartite conjunction of ear, sound and ear-consciousness, the last arising from the first two among which ear is the support and sound is the condition; that which is contact in relation to ear, ear- consciousness and sound, similar to that, the contact in present, past and future. This is called Contact by hearing.[84]

Contact by smelling is that which is contact due to tripartite conjunction of nose, smell and Olfactory consciousness, the last arising from the first two among which nose is the support and smell is the condition; that which is contact in relation to nose, nose-consciousness and smell, similar to that, the contact in present, past and future. This is called Contact by smelling.[85]

Contact by tasting is that which is contact due to tripartite conjunction of tongue, taste, and gustatory consciousness, the last arising from the first two among which tongue is the support and taste is the condition; that which is contact in relation to tongue, gustatory consciousness and taste, similar to that, the contact in present, past and future. This is called Contact by tasting.[86]

Tactile contact is that which is contact due to tripartite conjunction of body, touch, and body-consciousness, the last arising from the first two among which body is the support and touch is the condition; that which is contact in relation to body, body-consciousness and touch, similar to that, the contact in present, past and future. This is called Tactile contact.[87]

Mental contact is that which is contact due to tripartite conjunction of mind, object and mind-consciousness, the last arising from the first two among which mind is the support and object is the condition; that which is contact in relation to mind, mind-consciousness and object, similar to that, the contact in present, past and future. This is called Mental contact.[88]

10. SIX GROUPS OF FEELING

10.1 What is Feeling born of contact with eye ? That which is the feeling born of contact due to tripartite conjunction of (i) eye- consciousness arising from (ii) eye and (iii) material existence among which eye is the support, and material existence is the condition; in connection with eye, visual consciousness and material existence, that which is the feeling associated with Attention born of contact with eye; similar to that; every other feeling similar to that; that which is the feeling in past, future and present. This is called Feeling born of contact with eye.[89]

10.2. What is Feeling born of contact with ear, nose. tongue, body and mind ?

Feeling born of contact with ear is that which is born of contact due to tripartite conjunction of (i) ear-consciousness arising from (ii) ear and (iii) sound among which ear is the support, and sound is the condition; in connection with ear, ear- consciousness and sound, that which is the feeling associated with Attention born of contact with ear; similar to that, every other feeling similar to that; that which is the feeling in past, future, and present. This is called Feeling born of contact with ear.[90]

Feeling born of contact with nose is that which is born of contact due to tripartite conjunction of (i) olfactory consciousness arising from (ii) nose and (iii) smell among which nose is the support, and smell is the condition; in connection with nose, olfactory consciousness and smell, that which is the feeling associated with Attention born of contact with nose; similar to that, every other feeling similar to that; that which is the feeling in past, future and present. This is called Feeling born of contact with nose.[91]

Feeling born of contact with tongue is that which is born of contact due to tripartite conjunction of (i) gustatory consciousness arising from (ii) tongue and (iii) taste among which tongue is the support and taste is the condition; in connection with tongue, gustatory consciousness and taste, that which is the feeling associated with Attention born of contact with tongue; similar to that, every other feeling similar to that; that which is the feeling in past, future, and present. This is called Feeling born of contact with tongue.[92]

Feeling born of tactile contact is that which is contact due to tripartite conjunction of (i) body-consciousness arising from (ii) body and (iii) touch among which body is the support and touch is the condition; in connection with body, body-consciousness and touch, that which is the feeling associated with Attention born of tactile contact; similar to that, every other feeling similar to that; that which is the feeling in past, future and present. This is called Feeling born of tactile contact.[93]

Feeling born of mental contact is that which is contact due to tripartite conjunction of (i) mind-consciousness, (ii)mind and (iii) object among which mind is the support and object is the condition; in connection with mind, mind-consciousness and object, that which is the feeling associated with Attention born of mental contact; similar to that, every other feeling similar to that; that which is the feeling in past, future and present. This is called Feeling born of mental contact.[94]

II. SIX GROUPS OF NOTION

11.1. What is Notion born of visual contact ? The notion which is born of contact due to tripartite conjunction of (i) visual consciousness arising from (ii) eye and (iii) material existence among which eye is the support, material existence is the condition, in connection with eye, visual consciousness and material existence that which is notion associated with Attention born of contact with eye; similar, every other similar, similar in present, past and future. This is called Notion born of visual contact.[95]

11.2. What is Notion born of contact with ear, nose, tongue, and body ?

The Notion born of contact with ear is that which is born of contact due to tripartite conjunction of (i) ear consciousness arising from (ii) ear and (iii) sound among which ear is the support, sound is the condition; in connection with ear, ear-consciousness and sound that which is notion associated with Attention born of contact with ear, similar, every other similar, similar in present, past and future. This is called Notion born of contact with ear.[96]

The Notion born of contact with nose is that which is born of contact due to tripartite conjunction of (i) olfactory consciousness arising from (ii) nose and (iii) smell among which nose is the support and smell is the condition; in connection with nose, olfactory consciousness and smell that which is notion associated with Attention born of contact with nose, similar, every other similar, similar in present, past and future. This is called Notion born of contact with nose.[97]

The Notion born of contact with tongue is that which is born of contact due to tripartite conjunction of (i) gustatory consciousness arising from (ii) tongue and (iii) taste among which tongue is the support and taste is the condition; in connection with tongue, gustatory consciousness and taste that which is notion associated with Attention born of contact with tongue, similar, every other similar, similar in present, past and future. This is called Notion born of contact with tongue.[98]

The Notion born of tactile contact is that which is born of contact due to tripartite conjunction of (i) body consciousness arising from (ii) body and (iii) touch among which body is the support and touch is the condition; in connection with body, body- consciousness and touch that which is notion associated with Attention born of contact with body, similar, every other similar, similar in present, past and future notion. This is called Notion born of tactile contact.[99]

11.3 The Notion born of mental contact is that which is born of contact due to tripartite conjunction of (i) mind-consciousness arising from (ii) mind and (iii) object among which mind is the support and object is the condition; in connection with mind, mind- consciousness and object that which is notion associated with Attention born of contact with mind, similar, every other similar, similar in present, past and future. This is called Notion born of Mental contact.[100]

12. SIX GROUPS OF VOLITION

12.1 What is Volition born of contact with eye ? The volition which is born of contact due to tripartite conjunction of (i) visual consciousness arising from (ii) eye and (iii) material existence among which eye is the support and material existence is the condition; in connection with eye, visual consciousness and material existence that which is notion associated with Attention born of contact with eye; similar, every other similar,

similar in present, past and future. This is called Volition born of contact with eye.[101]

12.2 What is Volition born of contact with ear, nose, tongue and body ?

The Volition born of contact with ear is that which is born of contact due to tripartite conjunction of (i) ear-consciousness arising from (ii) ear and (iii) sound among which ear is the support and sound is the condition; in connection with ear, ear- consciousness and sound that which is volition associated with Attention born of contact with ear; similar, every other similar, similar volition in present, past and future. This is called Volition born of contact with ear.[102]

The Volition born of contact with nose is that which is born of contact due to tripartite conjunction of (i) olfactory consciousness arising from (ii) nose and (iii) smell among which nose is the support and smell is the condition; in connection with nose, olfactory consciousness and smell that which is volition associated with Attention born of contact with nose, similar, every other similar, similar in present, past and future. This is called Volition born of contact with nose.[103]

The Volition born of contact with tongue is that which is born of contact due to tripartite conjunction of (i) gustatory consciousness arising from (ii) tongue and (iii) taste among which nose is the support and tongue is the condition; in connection with tongue, gustatory consciousness and taste that which is volition associated with Attention born of contact with tongue; similar, every other similar, similar in present, past and future. This is called Volition born of contact with tongue.[104]

The Volition born of tactile contact is that which is born of contact due to tripartite conjunction of (i) body consciousness arising from (ii) body and (iii) touch among which body is the support and touch is the condition; in connection with body, body-consciousness and touch that which is volition associated with Attention born of contact with body; similar, every other similar, similar in present, past and future. This is called Volition born of tactile contact.[105]

12.3. The Volition born of mental contact is that which is born of contact due to tripartite conjunction of (i) mind consciousness arising from (ii) mind and (iii) object, mind being the support and object being the condition; in connection with mind, mind-consciousness and object that which is volition associated with Attention born of mental contact; similar, every other similar, similar in present, past and future. This is called Volition born of mental contact.[106]

13. SIX GROUPS OF CRAVING

13.1 What is Craving born of visual contact ? Craving which is born of feeling due to contact, contact is tripartite conjunction of (i) eye-consciousness arising from (ii) eye and (iii) material existence among which eye is the support, and material existence is the condition; in connection with eye, eye-consciousness and material existence that which is greed, similar, clinging, concealing, guarding, excessive pleasure is called Craving born of visual contact.[107]

13.2. What is Craving born of contact with ear, nose, tongue and body ?

Craving born of contact with ear is that which is born of feeling due to contact, contact is tripartite conjunction of (i) ear- consciousness arising from (ii) ear and (iii) sound among which ear is the support and sound is the condition; in connection with ear, ear-consciousness and sound that which is greed, similar, clinging, concealing, guarding, excessive pleasure is called Craving born of contact with ear.[108]

Craving born of contact with nose is that which is born of feeling due to contact, contact is tripartite conjunction of (i) olfactory consciousness arising from (ii) nose and (iii) smell among which nose is the support and smell is the condition; in connection with olfactory consciousness, nose and smell that which is greed, similar, clinging, concealing, guarding, excessive pleasure is called Craving born of contact with nose.[109]

Craving born of gustatory contact is that which is born of feeling due to contact, contact is tripartite conjunction of (i) gustatory consciousness arising from (ii) tongue and (iii) taste among which tongue is the support and smell is the condition; in connection with gustatory consciousness, tongue and taste that which is greed, similar, clinging, concealing, guarding, excessive pleasure is called Craving born of contact with tongue.[110]

Craving born of tactile contact is that which is born of feeling due to contact, contact is tripartite conjunction of (i) tactile consciousness arising from (ii) body and (iii) touch among which body is the support and touch is the condition; in connection with tactile consciousness, body and touch that which is greed, similar, clinging, concealing, guarding, excessive pleasure is called Craving born of tactile contact.[111]

13.3. Craving born of mental contact is that which is born of feeling due to contact, contact is tripartite conjunction of (i) mind-consciousness arising from (ii) mind and (iii) object among which mind is the support and object is the condition; in connection with mind-consciousness, mind and object that which is greed, similar, clinging, concealing, guarding, excessive pleasure is called Craving born of mental contact.[112]

NOTES

1. *Bhūmi* (ti, earth) signifies ' place of origin' *(gativiṣaya)* of *dharmas* (Cf. *AKB*, p. 186).

2. The *Prakaraṇapāda* (4th chapter) described four divisions of each with 10 varieties of the Mind-states whereas the *AK* takes up five divisions of the Mind- states. See *AK.* II, 23 with *AKB*.

3. For the meaning of the term *mahābhūmika (da-di-fa)* see *AKB*, *op. cit.* - The 'great earth' *(mahābhūmi)* means that it is the place of origin of *dharmas*. The *dharma* that is always found in the Mind stuff is called *mahābhūmika.*
Vibhāṣā (T.27 p. 80b8) suggests three meaning of the expression *mahābhūmikadharmas:-*
(a) Mind stuff is great; these ten *dharmas* are its *bhūmi*, the place of origin of the mind. Being the *bhūmi* of the great, these are called *mahābhūmi*. As these are *mahābhūmi* and *dharmas*, these are called *mahābhūmikadharmas.*
(b) The mind is great due to superiority of its nature and its activity; it is great and it is *bhūmi*, so it is *mahābhūmi*, being the place that serves as the support of the caittas. As the ten *dharmas vedanā* etc. are found everywhere in the *mahābhūmi*, these are named as the *mahābhūmikadharmas.*
(c) The ten *dharmas* are called 'great' *(tā)* as they are found everywhere with the mind. Being their *bhūmi*, the mind is called *mahābhūmi;* being inherent in the *mahābhūmi*, the *vedanā* etc. are named *mahābhūmikadharmas.*

4. The order of the ten *mahābhūmikadharmas* in the *AK* is different-*vedanā, cetanā saṃjñā, chanda, sparśa, mati, smṛti, manaskāra, adhimakṣa.* The order presented in the *AA* (p.66), however is closer to that of the *ADPS* the sole difference being the placement of *sparśa* before *cetanā.*

5. The Impure states, *mahākleśabhūmikadharmas (ta-fan-nao-ti-fa)* are the states which are born of all afflicted mental states *(sarvākuśalacittasahaja, AA*, p.66), the *AA* gives a list of ten *kleśamahābhūmikadharmas* in an almost similar order

with the *ADKPS*. The *AK*, however, explains only six kinds of the same.

6. According to the *AA*, the *kleśamahābhūmikadharmas are āśraddhya, kauśīdya, muṣitasmṛtitā, moha, mithyāmanaskāra, mithyādhimukti, auddhatya, avidyā* and *mithyāsaṃskāra*. The six *kleśamahābhūmikas* detailed in the *AK* are *moha, pramāda, kausīdya, āśraddhya, styāna and uddhava* (See II. 26.)

7. The Minor Impure state, *mahāparīttakleśabhūmikas (ta-hsiao-fan-nao-ti- fa)* are the mental states found in the sphere of small defilements (*parīttakleśa).*

8. According to the *AK* (II. 27), the ten *parīttakleśamahābhūmikas* are - *krodha, upanāha, śāṭhya, īrṣyā, pradāśa, mrkṣa, mātsarya, māyā, mada* and *vihiṃsā*. Compared to the list of the *ADKPS*, the *AA* includes *dveṣa, māna, mahāmāna* without mentioning *krodha, mada* and *vihiṃsā.*

9. The *kleśas (fan-nao*) are the mind-defiling factors that attach sentient beings to existence and thus causes bondage for them. Attachment *(rāga)* is one among the six *anuśayas* (proclivities)-*rāga, pratigha, māna, avidyā, dṛṣṭi,* and *vicikitsā*, For details see, *AK,* Ch. V.

10. *Dṛṣṭi (chien),* view, here refers to wrong and evil views which are mind-defiling factors causing hindrance to the attainment of pure knowledge. However, *dṛṣṭi* may also indicate right view or insight. Thus according to the *AKB* (II. 29) *dṛṣṭi* or view is a certain type of *prajñā* which 'takes across' *(sāṃtīrika)*. For details on wrong views in Pāli literature, see Nyanatiloka, *Buddhist Dictionary,* pp. 51-53. For varieties of *dṛṣṭi,* see S. Sastri, *Jñānaprasthāna,* pp. 7-9.

11. Five *kleśas* and Five *dṛṣṭis* enumerated in the *ADKPS* (1.5. 1.6; 3.1-4.5) are treated as the ten *saṃyojanas* (Fetter) in the Pāli and Sanskrit *Abhidharma* texts. *Saṃyojanas* are passions, the inclinations of the mind that bind beings to the wheel of existence. The noble individuals following the path leading to *Nirvāṇa,* must be free of the ten *saṃojanas.* In the Pāli *Nikāyas,* the list of the ten *saṃyojanas* include *māna* (Conceit), *uddhacca* (Restlessness), and *avijjā* (Ignorance) and omits *pratigha, antagrāhadṛṣṭi, dṛṣṭiparāmarśa,*

and *mithyādṛṣṭi* (see *AN, IV* 67, 68; X.13, *DN*, 33).
The *Vibha* (XVII) accepts *vyāpāda* (Ill-will), *māna, īrṣyā* (Envy), *mātsarya* (Avarice), and *avijjā* omitting *pratigha, satkāyadṛṣṭi, antagrāhadṛṣṭi, dṛṣṭiparāmarśa,* and including 'craving for existence' in place of *rūparāga* and *arūparāga.* Among the Sanskrit *Abhidharma* texts, the *Jñañaprasthānaśāstra* devotes its entire 2nd Chapter on the *saṃyojanas*. Five *kleśas and five dṛṣṭis* are discussed in the 4th section of the *Prakaraṇapāaśāstra*. In the *AK* (5th *Kośasthāthāna)*, the *saṃyojanas* are regarded as one of the five categories of *anuśaya* which are the "latent disposition of mind leading to evil volitions". However in the *AK* the *saṃyojanas* are nine in number-*anunaya* (Affection), *pratigha, māna, avidyā, dṛṣti, parāmarśa* (Unjustifying attachment), *vicikitsā, īrṣyā and mātsarya (AK.* V.17). The Five *dṛṣṭis* mentioned in the *AK.* V.7, are explained in details in the *AKB,* p. 772.

12. Contact, *ch'u (sparśa* literally *saṃsparśa)* is a basic mind state *(mahābhūmikadharma)*. In the *Therāvāda* tradition, it is a mental function described as an awareness bringing together mind and mental functions in such a way as if they 'touch' the object. Thus *saṃsparśa* is not an actual *dharma,* but an internal *dharma* functioning as a fundamental factor in cognitive process without a physical impact. This is the reason for which *saṃsparśa* belongs to the group of Mental Concomitants*(saṃskāraskandha)*.
Saṃsparśa is the seventh link in the chain of twelve links of Dependent origination. This is a situation when the six organs come in contact with their respective objects and consciousnesses. Thus there are six *saṃsparśas-cakṣusaṃsparśa, śrotrasaṃsparśa, ghrāṇasaṃsparśa, jihvāsaṃsparśa, kāyasaṃsparśa,* and *manaḥsaṃsparśa* (detailed in Section 9, *ADKPS)*. According to Vasubandhu, this is the stage of a child during the first two or three years after its birth when it cannot properly realize the feelings of pleasure, pain or indifference.

13. In general " Faculties' (*ken* in Chinese) refer to 22 partly physical and partly mental phenomena which have been detailed in the Pāli and the Sanskrit *Abhidharma*. Faculties are the conditions for the appearance or disappearance of feeling states. In the *ADPS* the five mental faculties of

feeling are treated as a separate category of elements technically known as "Five Faculties for feeling" *(vedanendriya).*

14. The classification of the Five *Dharmas* done in the *ADPS* is not seen in the Pāli and Sanskrit *Abhidharma* texts. In the *AK* II. 27, *vitarka* and *vicāra* are classified as *aniyata. Āhrīkya* and *anapatrāpya* are classified as *akuśalamahābhūmikas* (ii. 26.) , a category conceived in later *Ābhidharmiç* tradition (see *Vibhāṣā,* I.27, p. 220b4). *Vijñāna* refers to the six *vijñānakāyas.*

15. All conditioned *dharmas* are divided into five *skandhas- rūpa, vedanā, saṃjñā, saṃskāra* and *vijñāna.* These include all the physical and mental phenomena of existence *Vijñāna* is explained as the relative impression on the apprehension of each object. *Vijñānaskandha* indicates the formation of mind and its function. "The entire range of *vijñānaskandha"* is known as *mana-āyatana* (total Mind-base) consisting of seven *dhātus-* six *vijñañas (vijñañakāya* or *vijñañadhātu)* and *manodhātu* or the Mind, see. *AK.* I. 16; *AKB.* p. 50-51.

16. The six *saṃsparśas* mentioned as *pratighasparśa* in the section of Fivefold *sparśas* (i.7), are called *sparśakāyas.* The *sūtras* know the six *saṃsparśas* which are listed as a group in the Sūtra of the Hexades, *ṣaṭsaṭkodharmaparyāya,* See *MN,* iii. 180 (*Cacakkasutta*). However, in the *Therāvāda* tradition, *saṃsparśa* means the "coming together" of the mind, mental states and the object. The *Sarvāstivādins,* however, explains *sparśa* as "the result of coming together" *(saṃnipātaja)* of the object, sense organ and consciousness *(AK.* III, 21-22, 30). Thus the six *sparśakāyas* are regarded as separate *dharmas* in the *Sarvāstivāda Abhidharma.* The group of six contacts are listed in the *AA,* p123, *AVS.*5. The contact by mind-consciousness element (*manoviññānadhātusaṃphassa)* added to the six types mentioned above makes a list of seven types of contact in the *Vibh.* (18.1.10)

17. The *vedanāskandha* is divided into six kinds of feeling which are called *vedanākayas.* These are feelings produced by contacts with the organ of vision upto the feeling produced by contacts with the Mind-stuff. Cf. *AK.* I. 14 with *Sphutārthā.* The *Vibhaṅga* (18.1.11) enumerates seven types

of feeling-feeling born of eye-contact upto feeling born of mental contact, and feeling born of mind-consciousness element *(manoviññānadhātu)*.

18. The *saṃjñaśkandha,* like the *vedanāskandha* gives rise to six types of Notion which are called *saṃjñākāyas.* These are notions produced by contacts with the organ of vision upto the Notion produced by mental contact (*AK.* I.14). The *Vibh.* enumerates seven kinds of Notion (38.1.12).

19. The six types of Volition produced by the *cetanāskandha* are called *cetanākāyas* (see *AKB*, pp. 48-49). In The *Vibh,* seven types of *cetanā* are described with the addition of *manoviññānadhātusamphassajā cetanā* (Cf. 18.1.13).

20. The six types of Craving produced by the *saṃkāraskandha* are called *tṛṣṇākāyas.* The six *tanhākāyas* in the *Vibh* are - *rūpatanhā. saddatanhā, gandhatanhā, rasatanhā, phoṭṭhabbatanhā and dhammatanhā.*

21. The aspects of Feeling *(vedanā, shou)* presented here are the following:-
1. Feeling, one of the ten *mahābhūmikadharmas,* is a mental state of Feeling affection or experience *(anubhava).*
2. *Vedanā* is universally found in all beings *(sarvatraga).*
3. *Vedanā* includes all possible states' of feeling :
The detailed treatment of *vedanā* in other *Ābhidhārmic* sources points out that the nature of *vedanā* is experience *(anubhava,vitti)* by reason of perception of what is pleasant or painful or something distinct from both pleasure and pain. Thus there are three kinds of Feeling.
1. The experience of the agreeable characteristics of an object *(sukhāvedanā)* comforting the body and gladdening the mind.
2. The experience of the disagreeable characteristics of an object *(duḥkhavedanā)* disconcerting the body and the mind.
3. The experience of neutral characteristics causing neither discomfort nor comfort *(aduḥkhasukhavedanā)* to the body and the mind.
Vedanā is also characterized as enjoyment *(upabhoga)* as it enjoys the object either in whole or in its desirable form. With regard to sense - organs, *vedanā* is of six kinds (see *vedanākāya). Vedanā* is also treated as a separate *skandha* because it is the cause of the roots of dispute, cause *of*

transmigration, and also because of the grossness of feeling for which it is placed next to *rūpaskandha* in the order of the five *skandhas*, For details see *Dhs*. 3. *Atth*. III. 184-187, *SN* XXII, 55 *MN59; AK*. I. 21 and *AKB*, *AA* p. 66, *DS*, 22, 27; *MV* 100, 104.

Thirty Mind-states are listed under the head of *cittasaṃprayuktadharma* in *AA*. 6.12, 14,16; *DS*. 30; under the head of *caitasikadharma* in *Mvy*. 104; *Triṃśikā* 9-14, *Dhs*. i, *AK*. II. 23-27.

22. In the *ADPS*, Feeling and the next four *mahābhūmikadharmas* in the list of the ten basic states are defined in the same manner, in a style more common in the Pāli *Abhidharmma*. Thus Notion *(saṃjñā, hsiang)*, Volition, Contact, and Attention are defined as mental states which are universally found in all beings and include all possible states of Notion, Volition, Contact and Attention respectively. *Saṃjñā* is one of the five aggregates and is placed before *vijñāna*. It is the awareness of the common characteristics of an object. For details see *Dhas*. 4; *SN* XXII. 79. Also *AA*. 6.11 *vijñānāviśesāvalambanā saṃjñā* AK.1.14 *(samjñā nimittodgrahanātmikā*, *nimita*-charactristic mark, *udgrahaṇa*— determination).*Vijñānavāda*accepts later definition (*VHS*, p.20) and describes the activity of *saṃjñā* producing various names and concepts *(nānā-abhidhāna-prajñaptikarmikā)*.

23. Volition *(cetanā, ssu)* in its nature is action *(karmacetanā, AA. ibid; karmasvarūpa. AK, ibid.)*. *Sputārthā* (1.14) explains that *cetanā* conditions *(abhisaṃskāra)* the mind to create and act. It is *cittapraspanda* or "psychic stirring". The moral implication of *cetanā* is described in the *VMS, ibid*. - "its activity is to manoeuvre the mind towards the good etc... comprehending the characteristics of an object, it manoeuvres the mind to act in such a way that it produces good etc."

24. See F.N. 12. According to *Vijñānavādins*, Mental contact acts as the supporter (*saṃniśraya)* for the other four *caittas* i.e. *manaskāra, vedanā, saṃjñā* and *cetanā* (see *CWSL* 11b 19-20).

25. Attention (*manaskāra, tsuo-i)* is the rousing of the mind *(cetasa ābhoga)* so that it is directed towards its object (*AK*.

II. 24, *Sphutārthā; VMS, p.20). The AA.* 6.12 defines *manaskāra* as *cittāvismaraṇam* (mind tended to fix itself on the object).

26. Desire *(chanda, yü)* is one of the universal factors. It is essentially search for happiness *(hsin-ch'iu)* or willingness *(kartṛkāmyatā)* detailed in *Vibh.* 208; *AK.* II.24; *AKV; AA* 6.11; the *Vijñānavādins* explain *chanda* as a general factor as to wish for an object that is ardently desired *(abhipreta)*. For details see *VSM,* p. 20. The *CWSL* refutes the *Sarvāstivāda* position which asserts *chanda* as an universal factor.

27. Here Approbation *(adhimoksa, sheng-chiai)* is a *mahābhūmikadharma* universally found in all beings in all possible states of approval or approbation. *Adhimokkha* is mentioned in the list of *cetasikas* in *MN*III. As a *mahābhūmika, adhimokṣa* is also defined as a mind-state without obstruction (*cittasya anāvaraṇam, AA, Ibid,*) that is the determination of the object. According to *AK.* (II. 24) *adhimokṣa* is a general mental state, a "consideration of the object from the viewpoint of its qualities" *(tadālambanasya guṇatovadhāraṇāt, AKV.)*. When the *caittas* are born, they all approve the object and that is *adhimokṣa*. The *Yogācārins* define *adhimokṣa* (Resolution) as the decision and judgment *(avadhāraṇa)* regarding an object held with certainty, by the force of true or false teaching, of reasoning, of realization or evidence. There is no resolution regarding a thing which is not certain *(niścita)*. The *Yogācārins* argue that if the mind is not decided in regard to that thing, there is no resolution and thus *adhimokṣa* is not universal.

28. Memory *(smṛti, nien)* is a state of recollection *(i),* also recognized as that " which makes the mind remember clearly" *(abhilapanatā, VMS.* 25), and not forget *(pu-wang, asampromoṣa)* whatever has been experienced (see *AKV.* p. 187). According to the *Yogācārins, smṛti* serves as the support for meditation, because it retains the contents experienced in such a manner that there is no failure of recollection and thus it induces meditation *(CWSL,* 28b18-20).

29. Concentration *(samādhi, san-mo-ti)* is a *mahābhūmikadharma* refering to a fixed state *(sthiti, chu)* of mind because of which mind is totally united with its object *(AKV,* p. 187). It is non-distraction of mind *(cittasyācāñcalyaṃ, AA,* 6.11). According to the *Yogācārins,* in *samadhi,* the mind applies its whole concentration in examining the object of meditation. On the support of *samādhi,* the wisdom or the definite knowledge of the qualities etc. of the object is born (*CWSL* 28b25-30). For a detailed discussion on *samādhi* in the Pāli *Abhidhamma,* see Nyanatiloka, *op.cit.,* pp. 155-56.

30. That which is discrimination of the *dharmas (dharmapravicaya)* is designated as *mati* in the *AK* II. 24. In the *Ābhidhārmic* tradition, however, the term *prajñā* is also used to denote the same *(dharmavivekaḥ prajñā, AA, ibid.).* According to the Pāli *Abhidhamma, paññā* is Wisdom or Insight *(vipassanā)* which is the "intuitive knowledge which brings about the 4 stages of Holiness and the realization of *Nibbāna*" (Nyanatiloka, *op. cit.,* p. 122). *The Yogācārins* define *prajñā or dhī* as the discrimination of an object that is under examination (*upaparīkṣya*) and describes the activity of *prajñā* as elimination of doubt *(saṃśayavyāvartana).* For details, see *CWSL,* 28c 11-14.

31. Unbelief (*āśraddhya, pu-hsin*) is an impure state of mind which is defined here in *Abhidharma* style. The other *Ābhidhārmic* definitions of *āśraddhya* refer to the absence of liking (*cetaso prasādaḥ, AKV.* p. 191), Absence of faith in *dharma (cittasya dharme' nāvatāraḥ, AA* 6.15 etc. According to the *Yogācārins, āśradhya* is the defilement of mind that causes non-recognition (*anabhisaṃpratyaya), non-*desire *(anabhilāṣitva)* etc. in relation to the realities. Its activity is to oppose 'pure faith' and put a support for *kauśīdya (CWSL* 34b5-6).

32. Indolence *(kauśīdya, hsia-tai)* is the lack of energy in one's duty which is described in details under the head of "eight bases of laziness' *(kusittavatthu)* in the *Vibh.* According to the *AK* (II. 26, *AKV*), *Kauśīdya* is absence of activity *(nā bhyutsāha),* what is opposite to energy *(vīrya).* The *AA* (*ibid.*) defines *kauśīdya* as feeling tired in doing one's duty *(kṛtyeṣu cittapariśrāntiḥ). The Yogācārins* hold that *kauśīdya*

is one of the minor defilements which is by nature laziness in the cultivation of the good *dharmas* and the abandonment of the bad *dharmas (VMS.* pp. 31-32).

33. Forgetfulness (*muṣitasmṛtitā, shih-nien)* is a state of forgetting *(vismaraṇa).* The *AKV* on II. 23 examines why the five *dharmas* i.e., *muṣitasmṛti, vikṣepa, asamprajanya, ayoniśomanaskāra* and *mithyādhimokṣa* mentioned as *kleśamahābhūmikadharmas* in the *Jñañaprasthāna* (and also in the *ADKPS*) are not included in the list of *kleśamahābhūmikadharmas* in the *AK.* According to the *AKV* five *dharmas* have already been mentioned there as *mahābhūmikas* and it is unreasonable to name them again as *kleśamahābhūmikas.* Thus *muṣitasmṛtitā,* is nothing but defiled *smṛti, vikśepa* is defiled *samādhi, asamprajanya* is defiled *prajñā, ayoniśomanaskāra* is defiled judgment, and *mithyādhimokṣā* is defiled approbaion. The *Vijñānavādins* define *muṣitasmṛti* as the inability to remember the objects clearly *(kliṣṭā smṛtiḥ).* The activity of *muṣitasmṛti* is to counteract Right memory (*samyaksmṛti*) and to furnish the support for mental distraction *(vikṣepa).* Cf. *CWSL* 34b22-24

34. Distraction (*vikṣepa, hsin-luan*) is a defiled mental state in which the mind is not fixed into a single object. According to the *Yogācārins, vikṣepa* causes the mind to wander and disperse. It obstructs Right Meditation *(samyaksamādhi)* and furnishes the basis for bad discernment *(kuprajña)* CF. *VMS. ibid.*

35. *Avidyā* (Non-knowledge, *wu-ming*) is the absence of proper knowledge of three-world-elements- Sensuous world *(kāmadhātu),* the Fine-material world *(rūpadhātu),* and the Immaterial world *(arūpadhātu). Avidyā* is synonymous with Delusion *(moha)* and Ignorance *(ajñāna).* In *SN* XII. 4, *avijjā* is defined as 'not knowing the four truths, i.e., suffering, its arising, its cessation, and the way to its cessation". *Avidyā* is the first link in the formula of Dependent Origination *(pratītyasamutpāda)* as it is the root of all evil and suffering. It is also counted as one of the ten *saṃyojanas,* of the *āsavas* (cankers), and of the *anuśayas* (proclivities). For a critical study on the definitions on *avidyā* by the *Ābhidhārmikas* and the *Sautrāntiksas,* see *AKV,* pp. 463-67. According to the *Yogācārins, moha* is

error and obscurity so far as the principles of the things are concerned. Ignorance obstructs non-delusion and serves as the support for the defiled *dharmas*. Cf. *VMS. ibid.*

36. Non-discernment *(asamprajanya, pu-cheng-chih)* is identified with Ignorance in *Vibh.* 17.4.64. 104; *Pug, 34 (Aññaṇam. moho akusala-mulamasampajannam).* The *Vijñānavādins* define *asamprajanya* as 'inexact idea' (*viparīta buddhi*) of the object in consideration, that couneracts right understanding *(samprajanya)* and provokes transgression *(āpatti).*

37. Cf. *AK.* II. 26, *Sphutārthā,* p.190 - *manaskāra eva kliṣṭo yoniśomanaskāraḥ.* The *AA, op. cit.* mentions it as *mithyāmanaskāra* and defines it as "not remembering the path" (*mārgasya asmaraṇam).*

38. *Mithyādhimokṣa (hsieh-sheng-chieh)* is the non- abandonment of errors *(viparyāsāparityāga)* AA *ibid,* Also compare *adhimuktireva kliṣta mithyādhimokṣa iti (AK., ibid.).*

39. *Pu tsi-ching.*

40. *Auddhatya (tiao* - obstinate, *chu* - rash) is impatience of mind, giving way to vociferation *(hsiao).* Cf. *cittasya asthairyaṃ, AA. ibid.* According to the *Vijñañavādins, auddhatya* or *uddhava* is a state that causes the mind not to be peaceful to its object *(avyupaśama)* and it prevents equanimity and mental stillness *(śamatha),* see *CWSL* 34a 7-8.
In Pāli *Abhidhamma,* the state known as *uddhacco* is one of those mental factors inseparably associated with all unwholesome consciousness *(akuśala sādharaṇa).* It is one of the ten *saṃyojanas* and the five *nīvaraṇas.* See Nyanatiloka, *op. cit.,* p. *183.*

41. *Tuan fu-hai-fa (akuśalabhāvanāvipakṣa).*

42. Cf. *AKV,* p. 191- *pramādaḥ kuśalānāṃ dharmānāṃ abhavana.* The *Vijñānavādins* explain that the activity of *pramāda is to* "counteract vigilance *(apramāda),* to multiply *(vṛddhi)* the bad, and to ruin the good." *(VMS,* p.32*).*

43. Fury or *krodha (fen)* is listed first in the order of the ten *parītta kleśabhūmikadharmas* in the *AK* II. 27,. Again these ten *dharmas* are classified under the head of *upakleśa* (Secondary Defilements) in the *AK.* V.46. This classifica-

tion was later recognized by the *Vijñanavādins*. See *VMS*, p. 30. The list of *parīttas* in the *AA*. includes *Dveṣa (ibid)* in the place of *krodha* in its list of the ten *parīttas*. According to Pāli sources, Hatred is one of the unwholesome roots *(akuslamūla)* comprissing of *lobha* (Greed), *doṣa* (Hatred), and Delusion (*moha*). see *Vibh.*470The *Vijñānavādins* classify *krodha* under the category of *upakleśa* (Secondary Defilement). See. *VMS*. p. 30.

44. Enmity-*upanāha (hen)*. Cf. *AA, ibid. - katamaḥ upanāhaḥ manasa vipaktā sthitiḥ; VMS, ibid-upanāhaḥ vairānubandha* etc. *Upanāha* is "magnifying the object of irritation" *(āghātavastuvahulīkāra, AKB,* p. 846). The *VMS* explains that, as a result of Fury, (Cf. *pubbakālaṃ kodho aparakālaṃ upanāho,* p. 29), if the bad sentiments against somebody is not abandoned and the hostility is continued, then it is *upanāha* or Enmity. See *ibid.*

45. Hypocrisy (*mrakṣa, fu)* literally *yin-tui,* means "hiding crime or sin' *(pāpakartugopanaṃ AA ibid; avadyapraccādanaṃ, AA* p. 844, *VMS ibid.*). Also see PP., *ibid.* In the *VMS* the activity of *mrakṣa* is described as to obstruct non-dissimulation and to provoke affliction of remorse. In fact, one who hides his sin, is necessarily afflicted with remorse later on and loses feeling of tranquility.' *ibid.*

46. The description of Vexation *(pradāśa, nao)* here is similar to the *AA-adharmavastugrahaṇe tvarā* and *AKB,* p. 845 *sāvadyavastudṛḍhagrahīta.*
The *VMS* also explains *pradāśa* as a very angry state of mind (*ibid.*).

47. The definition of Envy (*īrṣyā, chi*) here is strikingly similar to that of the *AA - parasampad darśanād asahiṣṇutā (ibid.)* Cf. *AKB, ibid; VMS, ibid. (īrṣyā parasampattau cetaso vyāroṣah). For īrṣyā* in Pāli *Abhidhamma*, see PP p.30.

48. Parsimony *(mātsarya, chien)* is defined in the line of *AA-cittasya snehabhayād (dānakarmaṇi) apravṛttiḥ,* also *AKB., dharmāmiṣakauśalapradā avirodhī cittāgraho*. According to the *VMS* (*ibid.*) the activity of *mātsarya* is to obsturct non-parsimony and to provoke unkind feeling. For details in Pāli see *Vibh.* 17. 2. 51.

49. For further explanation of Deception *(sāṭhya, k' uang,* Pāli *saṭṭheya)* see *Vibh* 17.2.52 B; PP. 31, which describes it as the state of " fraud", " pretense", etc. or a person being associated with those states. *AKB, ibid,* and *VMS,* p.31 emphasizes the characteristics of 'crookedness' with regard to the state *(cittakautilyaṃ śāṭhyam).* Thus *śāṭhya* is to mislead others by not revealing the reality, distorting it, or making it obscure specially by pretending to be possessed of high qualities. *Śāṭhya* prevents frankness and provokes action leading to a 'depraved manner of life'.

50. Duplicity (*māya, cha'n*) is to 'mislead others' *(paravañcanā AKB,* p. 845) with crooked device which is described in details in *Vibh.* 17.2.52; *AA ibid.* According to the *Vijñānavādins* the activity of *māyā* is to prevent sincerity *(amāyā)* and moral exhortation *(avavāda).* With a view to mislead others, and in accordance with the circumstances, one uses various means to gain supremacy over the mind of the other person or to hide his own faults. Thereby he is capable to receive right exhortation from his teacher and friends. See VMS. pp. 30- 31.

51. The description of pride (*mada, chüeh)* here is similar to that of the *VMS* (p.31) and *AKB* II. 34. Thus *mada* is the exaltation of a person who produces a defiled attachment to his worldly prosperity *(svasampattau).* A proud person produces all kinds of impure *dharmas.* The *suttas* recognize three kinds of *mada*-pride in youth, pride in health, and pride in life and explain that being attached with the three kinds of pride, the ignorant worldly being persues an evil course in bodily action, speech and thought etc. See *DN* 33; *AN* III. 39 . A typical *Ābhidhārmic* definition is seen in the *Vibh.*

52. See *AKB, p. 846 (viheṭhanam vihiṃsā yena prahāra pārusyādibhiḥ parān viheṭhyate); VMS ibid*; *Vibh.* 23.4.95

53. Sensuous Attachment *(kāmarāga, yü-t'an).* According to Pāli *Abhidhamma* it is one of the ten *saṃyojanas,* (*AN* IV, 67, 68), sometimes classified as Attachment of Desire under four Attachments *(Vibh.)* and also as one of the four defilements *(ibid).* The *AKB,* (p. 731) classifies it under six or seven proclivities *(anuśaya)* as Attachment to desirable

objects *(kāmarāga)*. Compare the definition here to the *Vibh.*

54. Attachment for material existence (*rūparāga, se- t'an*) and Attachment for immaterial existence (*arūparāga, wu-se-t'an*) are also included in the category of the ten *saṃyojanas*. According to the *AKV*, p. 385, the Attachment to *rūpadhātu* and *arūpadhātu* is called *bhavarāga* (Attachment to existence), while *kāmarāga* is Attachment to desirable things that belong to *kāmadhātu*.

55. Hatred (*pratigha, ch'ien)* is synonymous with *vyāpāda* (Ill-will) *and dveṣa* or *doṣa* (Hatred). It is one of the six *anuśayas* (*AK*. V.I.). The definition here is close to that of the *Vibh.*

56. Doubt *(vicikitsā, i)* is one of the six *anuśayas,* one of the five Hindrances *(nīvaraṇa, AA*. p. 94). and one of the fetters *(saṃyojanas)*. According to *Dhā.* (1000) it is the sceptial doubt about the Buddha, the Teaching, the *Saṅgha,* the Training; about things past and future and conditionality. It is uncertainty *(yü)* as to whether things are bad or not, to be practiced or not etc. See. *Vibh.*17.
According to the *AA* (p. 78):-
1. *Vicikitsā* is the lack of decisive understanding as to whether " it exists or not", "it is or not", of a confused person who has not yet entered the path *(aprāptamārga)*.
2. *Rāga* is the sensuous attachment to all elements of confused person.
3. *Pratigha* is the violent agitation by anger in a confused mind over the undesirable happenings.

57. Personality - view *(satkāyadṛṣṭi, yu-sheng- chien)* is one of the ten *saṃyojanas*. For details, see *MN44; SN* XXII.1. According to *AKB*, p. 772 *'sat'* is that which perishes, and *'kāya'* is accumulation *(cayaḥ), satkāya* is the "accumulation of things perishing",. i.e., the five *upādānaskandhas, dṛṣṭ* is view. Thus *satkāyadṛṣṭi* means a 'view with regard to *satkā ya'*. The concept of *satkāya* is to discard the idea of permanence and the notion of unity. For details also see *Dhs* 1003. Five views are listed in *DS.* 68.

58. Viewpoint of eternalism or nihilism *(antagrāhadṛṣṭi, pien-chih-chien,* Takakusu refers to it as *kuo-chu* in *SAB* p. 110),

is a view that grasps extremes. It is to believe in the eternity (Pāli, *sāssata-diṭṭhi),* or in annihilation *(Pāli, uccheda-diṭṭhi).'* see *Vibh.* Also *AKB, ibid*; *AA.* p. 77 - *lokasyāsti antaḥ nāsti antaḥ ityevaṃ dṛṣṭir ucyate antagrāhadṛṣṭiḥ.* Also compare *VMS,* p. 63.

59. Wrong view *(mithyādṛṣṭi, hsieh-chien)* is the view of negating that which really exists, the Truth of Suffering etc., the view that rejects existence. All views are false but *mithyādṛṣṭi* is the most false of all. It is a negation *(apavādika),* others are attribution *(samāropika).* For details, see *AKB, ibid.* Also compare *AA, ibid.* - *catuḥsatyāni hetupratyayaḥ phalavipāka ityevaṃ dṛṣṭirucyate mithyādṛṣṭih.* For the *Vijñānavādins,* Wrong view perishes all kinds of vision *(sarvadarśanapāpavān),* see *VMS, ibid.*

60. *Dṛṣṭiparamarśa (chien-ch'u)* is the view which considers that which is 'low' or 'bad' *(hīna)* as 'good' (*AK,* p. 773). The 'low' is all that is defiled (*sāsrava*), because those are abandoned by the noble ones. Cf. *sāsravadharmeṣu vikalpayati satataṃ agrataṃ ityevaṃ dṛṣṭir ucyate dṛṣṭiparāmarśaḥ (AA, ibid.).* Cf. *VMS. (ibid)- dṛṣṭiparāmarśaḥ pañcasu upādānaskandheṣu agrato viṣiśtataḥ śreṣthataḥ paramataś ca yaddarśanaṃ.*

61. *Śilavrataparāmarśa (chiai-chin-ch'u)* is clinging (*upādāna*) to the *śīlas* (customs) and *brata* (rituals) as the ultimate truth. Cf. *Dhs.* 1215- " What is the clinging to mere Rules and Rituals ? The holding firmly to the view that through mere rules and rituals one may reach purification; this is called the clinging to mere rules and rituals." For the *Sarvāstivādins* it is that which is considering as cause that which is not cause, and as the Path that which is not the Path *(AKB, ibid.).* Cf. *AA.* p. 78-*aśucihetupratyayeṣu gaveṣayati pariśuddhimārgaṃ ityevaṃ dṛṣṭir ucyate śilavrataparāmarśaḥ.* According to the *Vijñānavādins,* it is considering the five *upādānaskandhas* as of being pure, free and transcending the spheres of limited existence *(VMS* p. 64).

62. *Pratighasaṃsparśa (yu-tui-ch'u)* as described here are the five classes of contact by senses, i.e., visual contact, contacts by hearing, smelling, tasting, and tactile contact. These are called *pratighasaṃsparśa* as they have got the contactable (*sapratigha*) organs as their support. For details, see *AKB,*

p. 471. *MN*9. adds mental contact with fivefold contacts and admits six classes of contact by senses.

63. *Adhivacanasaṃsparśa (tseng-yu-ch'u)* or Mental contact is that which properly designates *(adhivacana)* the object of *sparśa* associated with *manovijñāna*. The other explanation is that only the *manovijñāna* is activated with regard to its object with expression or speech *(adhikṛtya vacanaṃ), and* thus *manovijñāna* is *adhivacana*. The contact associated with it is called *adhivacanasaṃsparśa*. For details see *AKB, ibid.* In *DN*15 and *AA,* p. 71 the twofold division of physical and mental contact *paṭighasamphassa* and *adhivacana samphassa* is mentioned.

64. *Vidyāsaṃsparśa (ming-ch'u)* is pure *adhivacanasaṃsparśa,* as the latter is associated with pure knowledge *(vidyā)*. For details see *AK*. III. 31 with *AKV*, p. 472.

65. According to the *AKB, avidyāsaṃsparśa (wu-ming- ch'u)* is impure mental contact *(kliṣṭo vidyāsaṃsparśa)* when associated with both knowledge and ignorance *(vidyā 'vidyābhyāṃ samprayuktatvāt, ibid.)*.

66. *Naivavidyā- nāvidya-saṃsparśa (fei-ming-fei- wu-ming ch'u)* is indifferent mental contact as it is not associated with *vidyā* or *avidyā*. It is associated with only good *(kuśala)* but impure (*sāsrava)* knowledge. For details, see *ibid.* For five contacts also see *AA,* p. 133.

67. According to the *AKB* (p. 138), the five Faculties for Feeling, i.e. *sukha, duḥkha, saurmanasya, daurmanasya,* and *upekṣā* are called Faculties or *indriya* (predominating factor) regarding contamination (*saṃkleśa*) as the proclivities (*anuśayas*) like attachment, hatred, delusion etc. become attached to the Faculties for feeling and entangle beings in worldly bondages. The cessation of the five Faculties is enumerated in the *AK*. p. 145-46; *AA,* p. 129 etc.

68. *Sukhendriya (lo-ken)* is the bodily *(kāyīki)* agreeable *(śātā)* feeling (*vedana*). In the third *dhyāna,* however the favorable feeling is mental and not physical. See *AKB,* p. 146; *Vibh.* p. 158 etc.

69. *Duḥkhendriya (k'u-ken)* is bodily disagreeable feeling (*AKB,* p. 145). Compare the definition here with *Vibh. ibid.*

70. *Saurmanasyendriya (hsi-ken)* is defined here in the line of the *Vibh, ibid.* The *AKB* describes it as a mentally agreeable feeling in the world of desire (*kāmadhātu*), and in the first and second *dhyānas* (see *ibid*).

71. *Dauramanasyendriya (yu-ken).* Cf. *Vibh. ibid.* According to *AKV (ibid),* it is a disaggreable *(asātā)* mental feeling.

72. *Upekṣendriya (she-ken).* Cf. *Vibh., ibid.* The *AKB* holds that this is intermediate *(madhya),* as it is neither agreeable nor disagreeable (see p. 147).

73. *Vitarka (hsin)* in the *Vibh* (p.308) is defined as "mentation, thinking, thought, fixation, focussing, application of the mind, right thought. This is called initial application" *(vitakka),* Tr. *The Book of Analysis,* p. 335. The *AKB* (p. 204) defines it as crudeness of mind (*cittaudārikatā*) which is not yet fixed at its object. According to the *Vijñañavādins,* it is indistinct murmur of the mind *(manojalpa)* which is searching *(paryeṣaka)* after its object. It is a mental activity in which the mind proceeds with a discernment *(prajña)* of good and evil. For details, see *VMS,* p. 33.

74. *Vicāra (tzu)* is defined here in the line of the *Vibh* (p. 309). Also compare AA (p. 94)-*cittasya udgṛhītasaṃskārānucintanaṃ ucyate vicāraḥ.* According to the *AKB* (p. 204), compared to *vicāra, vitarka* is a subtle understanding of abstract thought that occurs together with *vicāra.* The *Vijñañavādins* explain that *vicāra* is also a *manojalpa* which attempts to fix *(pratyavekṣaka)* its object. Thus as it involves ascertainment *(nirūpaṇa)* of what was understood earlier *(pūrvādhigata),* it is called subtlety *(sūkṣmatā). Vicāra* provides a basis for what is agreeable to senses and what is not. For details, see *VMS, ibid.*

75. *Āhrikaya (wu-tsan).* In Pāli *Abhidhamma*, it is one of the four unwholesome factors associated with unwholesome states of consciousness. Cf. *Vibh.* p. 429 tr:- "That which is not having shame where there should be shame, not having shame at the attaining of evil states." It is " lack of moral shame" (*ANII. 6; PP.* p. 59; *Dhs.* 387; *Vibh.* 429 etc.); also compare *AB.* (p.201-2) - *ahrīraguruta* which means that *āhrīkya* is the absence of respect to the teacher. It is also the absence of shame and lack of self-respect. For

the *Vijñānavādins,* it is disregard to oneself and the *dharma.* It counteracts the sense of shame, produces and nourishes bad actions. Cf. *VMS,* p. 31.

76. *Anapatrāpya (wu-k'uei)* is defined in the *Vibh., ibid.* "that which is not having fear of blame *(ottappa)* where there should be fear of blame....etc. According to *AKB (ibid),* it is that which is lack of fear of being condemned by others for doing wrong *(avadye bhayāadarśitvaṃ).* The *Vijñānavādins* hold that *anapatrāpya* is disregard to self and respect for violence and evil, having no sense of shame for his sins. It opposes integrity, producing and nourishing all evil actions. The difference between *āhrīkya* and *anapatrāpya* is stated in the *AA* (p. 81)-*āhrīkya* is the lack of internal shame for one's evil doings *(duṣkṛte nātmani lajjā)* and *anapatrāpya* is the lack of sense of being condemned by others *(duṣkṛte na parato lajjā).*

77. *Cakṣurvijñāna (yen-shih).* According to the *AKV*(55) it is a mental function resulting in a contact between material existence *(rūpa)* and eye *cakṣu),* the first being dependent on the second that is the condition *(ālambana)* and on the third that is the support *(āśraya).* Cf. *AK.* 17 with *AKB* and *AKV* on it; *Vibh.* p. 109; *AA.* 54; *CWSL* 26a16-23. The five *vijñānakāyas* are always impure and it comprises *manovijñāna* when it becomes impure. See Poussin *AK* I, p. 51.

78. *Śrotravijñāna (erh-shih)* is the resultant consciousness, sound being its *ālambana* and the ear being its *āśraya.* see *AKB, AKV., ibid; Vibh, ibid; AA. ibid.*

79. *Ghrāṇavijñāna (pi-shih)* is the resultant consciousness, *gandha* being its *ālambana* and the nose being its *āśraya.* See *ibid.*

80. *Jihvāvijñāna (she-shih)* is the resultant consciousness, *rasa* being its *ālambana* and the tongue being its *āśraya.* See *Vibh.,* p. 110.

81. *Kāyavijñāna (shen-shih)* is dependent on *sprastavya* that is *ālambana* and the body that is *āśraya.* See *ibid.*

82. *Manovijñāna* (*i-shih*) arises in contact with *dharmadhātu* as *ālambana* and *manodhātu* as *āśraya.* See *ibid.*

83. *Cakṣusaṃsparśa (yen-ch'u)*. See f. n. 12. The six divisions of contact (*sparśakāya*) born of tripartite conjunction *(tṛkasaṃnipāta)* of the sense-organ that is *āśraya*, of the object that is *ālambana,* and of the consciousness (*vijñāna*), are also known to the *Sūtra of the six Hexades (ṣaṭṣaṭako dharmaparyāya*). *MN.* iii.180. The *Ābhidhārmikas* recognize the six contacts as separate *dharmas*. According to the *Sarvāstivādins, saṃnipāta* (conjunction) means " the result of conjunction." Thus *sparśa* is that which is "born of conjunction of the three" mentioned earlier. However, the *Vijñānavādins* hold that *sparśa* is " conjunction of the three". For details, see Guenther (Delhi, 1974), pp. 33-34. For *sparśakāyas,* see *AA*. p. 123, *AVS* 5; *AK* III. 21-22 with *AKB*.

84. *Śrotrasaṃsparśa (erh-ch'u)*. Cf. *Budd. Manual,* p. 178.

85. *Ghraṇasaṃsparśa (pi-ch'u)*. Cf. *ibid.,* p. 180.

86. *Jihvāsaṃsparśa (she-ch'u)*. Cf. *ibid.,* p. 181

87. *Kāyasaṃsparśa (shen-ch'u)*. *Ibid.*, p. 182.

88. *Manaḥsparśa (i-ch'u)*. In the *Ābhidhārmic* tradition, name *(adhivacana)* is the object of contact associated with mental consciousness- " through the Visual consciousness, one knows blue; but one does not know "It is blue"; through the mental consciousness, one knows blue and one knows, 'it is blue'." quoted in the *AKB,* p. 472.

89. *Cakṣusaṃsparśajā vedanā (yen-ch'u-suo- sheng-shou)*. The *Aṭṭh* (III.183) mentions that *sparśa* produces feeling. The *Vaibhāṣikas* maintain that *sparśa* and *vedanā* are simultaneous, whereas the *Sautrāntika* holds that *vedanā* is later than *sparśa*. For details, see *AKV* (p. 473-76). According to *AK,* this is a physical feeling. The definitions here demonstrate a typical *Ābhidhārmic* style of the *Sarvāstivādins-* this feeling is born of conjunction of eye, *rūpa* and visual consciousness, it is found in all beings in all times. The *Vibh.* (p. 32) mentions the sixfold division of the aggregate of Feeling.

90. *Śrotrasaṃsparśajā vedanā (erh-ch'u-suo- sheng-shou)* is feeling born of ear, sound, and ear- consciousness, that which is found in all beings in all times.

91. *Ghrāṇasaṃsparśajā vedanā (pi-ch'u- suo-sheng-shou)* is feeling born of nose, smell, and olfactory consciousness, that which is found in all beings in all times.

92. *Jihvāsaṃsparśajā vedanā (she-ch'u-suo- sheng-shou)* is feeling born of conjunction of tongue, taste, and gustatory consciousness, that which is found in all beings in all times.

93. *Kāyasaṃsparśajā vedanā (shen-ch'u-suo- sheng-shou)* is feeling born of conjunction of body, touch and tactile consciousness that which is found in all beings in all times.

94. *Manaḥsaṃsparśajā vedanā (i-ch'u-suo- sheng-shou)* is feeling born of conjunction of mind, object and mind-consciousness that which is found in all beings in all times.

95. *Cakṣusaṃsparśajā saṃjñā (yen- ch'u-suo-sheng-hsiang)* is notion dependent on conjunction of visual consciousness, eye and material existence, that which is found in all beings in all times.

96. *Śrotrasaṃsparśajā saṃjñā (erh-ch'u-suo-sheng-hsiang)* is notion dependent on conjunction of ear-consiousness, ear and sound, that which is found in all beings in all times.

97. *Ghrāṇasaṃsparśajā saṃjñā (pi-ch'u-suo-sheng-hsiang)* is notion dependent on conjunction of olfactory consciousness, nose and smell, that which is found in all beings and exists in all times.

98. *Jihvāsaṃsparśajā saṃjña (she-ch'u-suo-sheng-hsiang)* is notion resulting from conjunction of gustatory consciousness, tongue and taste, that which is found universally in all times.

99. *Kāyasaṃsparśajā saṃjñā (shen- ch'u-suo-sheng-hsiang)* is notion resulting from conjunction of tactile consciousness, body and touch, that which is found in all beings in all times.

100. *Manaḥsaṃsparśajā saṃjñā (i- ch'u-suo-sheng-hsiang)* is notion resulting from conjunction of mind-consciousness, mind and object, that which is found in all beings in all times.

101. *Cakṣusaṃsparśajā cetanā (yen-ch'u-suo- sheng-szu)* is volition arising from conjunction of visual consciousness, eye and material existence, that which is assoicated with *manas*

are born of visual contact, and found in all beings in all times.

102. *Śrotrasaṃsparśajā cetanā (erh-ch'u-suo- sheng-szu)* is volition dependent on ear consciousness, ear and sound--- of contact by hearing---.

103. *Ghrāṇasaṃsparśajā cetanā (pi-ch'u- suo-sheng-szu)* is volition dependent on olfactory consciousness, nose and smell.. of contact by smelling....

104. *Jihvāsaṃsparśajā cetanā (she-ch'u-suo- sheng-szu)* is volition dependent on gustatory consciousness, tongue and taste... of contact by tasting...

105. *Kāyasaṃsparśajā cetanā (shen-ch'u-suo- sheng-szu)* is volition dependent on tactile consciousness, body and touch.. of contact by touching...

106. *Manaḥsaṃsparśajā cetanā (i-ch'u-suo- sheng-szu)* is volition dependent on mental consciousness, mind and object.. of contact by mind...

107. *Cakṣusaṃsparśajā tṛṣṇā (yen-ch'u-suo-sheng-ai)* is craving produced by visual consciousness, eye and material existence.. is greed etc.. found in all beings.

108. *Śrotrasaṃsparśajā tṛṣṇā (erh-ch'u-suo-sheng-ai)* is craving produced by ear- consciousness, ear and sound.. is greed etc.. found in all beings.

109. *Ghrāṇasaṃsparśajā tṛṣṇā (pi-ch'u-suo-sheng-ai)* is craving produced by olfactory consciousness, nose and smell...in greed etc. ...found in all beings.

110. *Jihvāsaṃsparśajā tṛṣṇā (she-ch'u-suo-sheng-ai)* is craving produced by gustatory consciousness, tongue and taste... is greed etc... found in all beings.

111. *Kāyasaṃsparśajā tṛṣṇā (shen-ch'u-suo-sheng-ai)* is craving produced by tactile consciousness, body, and touch... is greed etc. .. found in all beings.

112. *Manaḥsaṃsparśajā tṛṣṇā (i-ch'u-suo sheng-ai)* is craving produced by mind-consciousness, mind and object ... is greed etc. ... found in all beings.

CHAPTER II

MINOR DIVISIONS

ASSOCIATED AND NOT ASSOCIATED

II.1.0. The Chapter discusses 88 categories. The first three categories are (1) Feeling, (2) Groups of Consciousness and the (two *dharmas*) of (3) Absence of sense of shame and Absence of fear of blame. The remaining 85 categories are Feeling etc., associated[1] and not associated[2] (with reference to) a series of Elements, Bases and Aggregates.

1. FIVE FACULTIES FOR FEELING AND OTHER STATES

II.1.1. Five Faculties for Feeling are - (1) Faculty for Feeling pleasure, (ii) Faculty for Feeling pain, (iii) Faculty for Feeling satisfaction, (iv) Faculty for Feeling dissatisfaction, and (v) Faculty for Feeling indifference.[3]

II. 1.2. The Basic mind-state of Feeling, is associated with how many of the fivefold Faculties for Feeling ? With how many is it not associated and thus until 'Craving born of mental Contact', is associated with how many of the fivefold Faculties for Feeling ? With how many is it not associated?

II. 1.3. The Basic mind-state of Feeling is not associated with any of the five Faculties of Feeling. The Basic mind state of Notion is associated with all of the five Faculties for Feeling. Likewise, Volition, Contact, Attention, Desire, Approbation, Memory, Concentration, and Discernment are associated with all of the five Faculties for Feeling.[4]

II. 1.4. Unbelief is not associated with the five Faculties. Likewise, the remaining Impure mind-states are not associated with the five Faculties.[5]

II. 1.5. Fury, Enmity, Vexation, Envy and Harmfulness are associated with two Faculties, i.e., those of dissatisfaction and indifference. Hypocrisy, Duplicity and Deception are associated with only three Faculties other than those of pleasure and pain. Pride is associated with four Faculties other than that of pain. Parsimony is associated with only two Faculties, i.e., those of satisfaction and indifference.[6]

II.1.6. Sensuous Attachment and Attachment for material existence are associated with the three Faculties other than those of pain and dissatisfaction. Attachment for Immaterial existence is associated with a single Faculty, i.e., that of indifference. Hatred is associated with the three Faculties other than those of pleasure and satisfaction. Doubt is associated with the four Faculties other than that of pain.

II.1.7. Among five Views, False View is associated with the four Faculties other than that of pain. The remaining four Views are associated with the three Faculties other than those of pain and dissatisfaction.[7]

II. 1.8. Contact by sensorial reaction is associated with the three Faculties other than those of satisfaction and dissatisfaction. Verbal Contact is associated with the four Faculties other than that of pain. Contact by knowledge is associated with the three Faculties other than those of pain and dissatisfaction. Contact by ignorance upto Contact by neither-knowledge-nor-non-knowledge are associated with none of the five Faculties.[8]

II. 1.9. Searching state of mind and Investigation are associated with the two Faculties, i.e., those of pain and dissatisfaction, are not associated with the other three Faculties. Consciousness is associated with all of the five Faculties. Absence of sense of shame, and Absence of fear of blame are associated with all of the five Faculties.[9]

II. 1.10. Eye-consciousness is associated with the three Faculties, i.e., those of pleasure, pain, and indifference. Likewise, Ear-consciousness, Olfactory consciousness, Gustatory consciousness, and Tactile consciousness are associated with those three Faculties. Mind-consciousness is associated with the four Faculties, i.e., those of pleasure, satisfaction, dissatisfaction, and indifference.[10]

II. 1.11. Six Groups of Contact, six Groups of Notion, six Groups of Volition are associated with the Faculties for satisfaction and dissatisfaction, not associated with other three Faculties.[11]

II. 1.12. Feeling born of visual contact is not associated with any of the five Faculties for Feeling. The remaining Groups of Feeling and also Craving born of visual contact are associated with two of the five Faculties, i.e., those for pleasure and indifference. Like Craving born of visual contact, the other Cravings born of contact with ear, nose, tongue, body, and also Craving born of mental contact are associated with the three of the Faculties, i.e., those for pleasure, satisfaction and indifference.

2. SIX GROUPS OF CONSCIOUSNESS AND OTHER STATES

II. 2.1. Six Groups of Consciousness are Visual Consciousness, Ear-consciousness, Olfactory Consciousness, Gustatory Consciousness, Tactile Consciousness and Mind-Consciousness.

II. 2.2. The Basic mind-state of Feeling, is associated with how many of the six Groups of Feeling? With how many is it not associated and upto Craving born of mental contact is associated with how many of the six Groups of Consciousness ? With how many it is not associated ?

II. 2.3. The Basic mind-state of Feeling is associated with all of the six Groups of Consciousness. Like the Basic mind-state of Feeling, the remaining Basic mind-states are associated with all of the six Groups of Consciousness.

II.2.4. Unbelief is not associated with the six Groups of Consciousness. Like Unbelief, the remaining Impure states are not associated with the six Groups of Consciousness.

II. 2.5. Fury is associated only with Mind-Consciousness. Like Fury, the remaining Minor Impure states are associated only with Mind-consciousness.

II. 2.6. Sensuous Attachment is not associated with six Groups of Consciousness. Like Sensuous Attachment, Hatred is not associated with the six Groups of Consciousness. Attachment for Material existence is associated with the four Groups of Consciousness other than those of Olfactory Consciousness and Gustatory Consciousness. Attachment for Immaterial existence and Doubt are associated only with Mind-consciousness.

II. 2.7. Five Views are associated only with Mind-Consciousness.

II.2.8. Contact by sensorial reaction is associated with the five Groups of Consciousness, not associated with Mind consciousness. Verbal or Mental Contact is associated only with Mind-consciousness, not associated with the five Groups of Consciousness. Contact by knowledge is associated only with Mind- consciousness. Contact by ignorance and Contact by neither- knowledge-nor-non-knowledge is not associated with the six Groups of Consciousness.

II. 2.9. Faculty of pleasure is associated with six Groups of Consciousness. Faculty of indifference is not associated with six Groups of consciousness. Faculty of pain is associated with the five Groups of Consciousness other than that of Mind- consciousness.

II.2.10. Searching state of mind and Investigation are associated with six Groups of Consciousness but not with Mind-Consciousness.

II. 2.11 Consciousness *dharma* is not associated with six Groups of consciousness.

II.2.12. Absence of sense of shame and Absence of fear of blame are not associated with six Groups of Consciousness.

II.2.13. Eye-consciousness is not associated with six Groups of consciousness. Like Eye-consciousness, Ear-consciousness, Olfactory Consciousness, Gustatory Consciousness, Tactile Consciousness and Mind-consciousness are not associated with six Groups of consciousness.

II. 2.14 Visual Contact is associated with one Group of consciousness, that is Eye-consciousness, is not associated with five Groups of consciousness other than Eye-consciousness. Like Visual Contact, Contacts by ear, nose, tongue, body and mind are associated with Ear-consciousness, Olfactory Consciousness, Gustatory Consciousness, Tactile Consciousness and Mind- consciousness respectively.

II. 2.15 Like six Groups of Contact are six Groups of Feeling, six Groups of Notion, six Groups of Volition and the like.

II.2.16. Craving born of visual contact is associated only with Eye-consciousness. Like Craving born of visual contact, Craving born of contact by ear, nose, tongue, body and mind are associated with Ear-consciousness,

Olfactory Consciousness, Gustatory Consciousness, Tactile Consciousness and Mind-consciousness respectively.

3. ABSENCE OF SENSE OF SHAME AND ABSENCE OF FEAR OF BLAME AND OTHER STATES

II. 3.1. Two *Dharmas*-Absence of sense of shame and Absence of fear of blame.

II. 3.2. The Basic mind-state of Feeling, is associated with how many of the two *Dharmas*? From how many is it not associated and thus until 'Craving born of mental contact', is associated with how many of those two *Dharmas*? From how many is it not associated?

II. 3.3. Of Basic mind-State of Feeling , those which are impure, are associated with those two *Dharmas*. The remaining states of Feeling are not associated. Like Basic mind-state of Feeling, are the remaining Basic mind-states.

II. 3.4. Of Unbelief that which is impure is associated with the two *Dharmas*. The remaining Unbelief is not associated with the two *Dharmas*. Like Unbelief are the remaining Impure states.

II. 3.5. Fury, Enmity, Hypocricy, Vexation, Envy, Parsimony and Harmfulness are associated with the two *Dharmas*. Of Duplicity, Deception and Pride, those which are impure are associated with the two *Dharmas*. Remaining Duplicity, Deception and Pride are not associated with the two *Dharmas*.

II. 3.6. Greed for Material existence and Greed for Immaterial existence are not associated with the two *Dharmas*. Of Doubt that which is impure is associated with two *Dharmas*. Remaining Doubt is not associated with two *Dharmas*.

II. 3.7. Of five Views, two Views are not associated. Of three Views those which are impure are associated with two *Dharmas*. Remaining three Views are not associated.

II.3.8. Of Contact by Sensorial reaction, Verbal Contact and Contact by ignorance, those which are impure, are associated with two *Dharmas*. Other three Contacts are not associated. Contact by knowledge and Contact by neither knowledge-nor-non-knowledge are not associated.

II.3.9. Of Faculty for pleasure, that which is impure, is associated with two *Dharmas*. Other Faculty of pleasure is not associated. Like Faculty of pleasure are Faculties of pain, satisfaction, dissatisfaction and indifference.

II.3.10 Of Searching state of mind Investigation, and Consciousness, those which are impure, are associated with two *Dharmas*. Other Searching state of mind Investigation and Consciousness are not associated with two *Dharmas*. Absence of sense of shame is not associated with two *Dharmas*. Absence of fear of blame is also not associated with two *Dharmas*.

II. 3.11. Of Visual Consciousness that which is impure, is associated with two *Dharmas*. Other Visual Consciousness is not associated. Like Visual Consciousness are Ear-Consciousness, Olfactory Consciousness, Gustatory Consciousness, Tactile Consciousness and Mind-consciousness.

II. 3.12. Like six Groups of Consciousness are six Groups of Contact, six Groups of Notion, Six Groups of Volition etc.

II. 3.13. Of Cravings born of contacts by eye, ear, body and mind, those which are impure, are associated with two *Dharmas*. Other Cravings born of contacts by eye, ear, body and mind are not associated with two *Dharmas*. Craving born of contacts by nose and tongue are associated with two *Dharmas*.

At the end of *chüan* I it is said : The *Dhātukāyapādaśāstra* belongs to the *Sarvāstivāda* School.

INCLUDED AND EXCLUDED CONCERNING ASSOCIATED AND NOT ASSOCIATED

4. FEELING AND OTHER STATES

II. 4.1. That which is associated with Feeling, that which is not associated with Notion; (under) 18 elements, 12 bases and 5 aggregates, that which is associated with Feeling is included in what ? In Mind-state and Mental state, 8 elements, 2 bases and 3 aggregates. What is that which is left over ? Feeling, Material existence, Unconditioned and Mind-dissociated impressions; that is to say 11 elements, 11 bases and 3 aggregates.

That which is not associated with Notion is included in what ? In Notion, Material existence, Unconditioned, and Mind-dissociated impressions; that is to say, 11 elements, 11 bases and 3 aggregates.

II. 4.2. That which is associated with Notion, that which is not associated with Feeling; (under) 18 elements, 12 bases and 5 aggregates, that which is associated with Notion is included in what ? In Mind-state and Mental state, 8 elements, 2 bases and 3 aggregates. What is that which is left over ? Notion, Material existence, Unconditioned and Mind-dissociated impressions; That is to say 11 elements, 11 bases and 3 aggregates.

That which is not associated with Feeling is included in what? In Feeling, Material existence, Unconditioned and Mind-dissociated impressions; that is to say, 11 elements, 11 bases and 3 aggregates.

II.4.3. As Feeling paired with Notion is explained, in the same way upto Feeling paired with Discernment are to be explained.

II. 4.4. That which is associated with Feeling, that which is not associated with Unbelief; (under) 18 elements, 12 bases and 5 aggregates that which is associated with Feeling is included in what ? In Mind-state and Mental state, 8 elements, 2 bases and 3 aggregates. What is that which is left over? Feeling, Material existence, Unconditioned and Mind-dissociated impressions; that is to say 11 elements, 11 bases and 3 aggregates.

That which is not associated with Unbelief is included in what? In Unbelief, Material existence, Unconditioned and Mind- impression; That is to say, 18 elements, 11 bases and 3 aggregates.

II. 4.5. That which is associated with Unbelief, that which is not associated with Feeling; (under) 18 elements, 12 bases and 5 aggregates that which is associated with Unbelief is included in what? In Mind-state and Mental state, 8 elements, 2 bases and 4 aggregates. What is that which is left over? Unbelief, Material existence, Unconditioned and Mind-dissociated impressions; that is to say, 18 elements, 12 bases and 5 aggregates.

That which is not associated with Feeling is included in what? In Feeling, Material existence, Unconditioned, and Mind-dissociated impressions; that is to say, 11 elements, 11 bases, and 3 aggregates.

II.4.6. As Feeling paired with Unbelief is explained, in the same way upto Feeling paired with the rest of the Impure states, Sensuous Attachment, Hatred, Contact by ignorance, Contact by neither-knowledge-nor-non-knowledge, Absence of sense of shame, and Absence of fear of blame are to be explained.

II.4.7. That which is associated with Feeling, that which is not associated with Fury; (under) 18 elements, 12 bases and 5 aggregates, that which is associated with Feeling is included in what ? In Mind-state and Mental state, 8 elements, 2 bases and 3 aggregates. What is that which is left over? Feeling, Material existence, Unconditioned and Mind-dissociated impressions; that is to say, 11 elements. 11 bases and 3 aggregates.

That which is not associated with Fury is included in what ? In Fury, Material existence, Unconditioned and Mind-dissociated impressions; that is to say, 18 elements, 12 bases and 5 aggregates.

II.4.8. That which is associated with Fury, that which is not associated with Feeling; (under) 18 elements, 12 bases, and 5 aggregates, that which is associated with Fury is included in what ? In Mind-state and Mental state, 3 elements, 2 bases and 4 aggregates. What is that which is left over? Fury, Material existence, Unconditioned and Mind-dissociated impressions; that is to say 18 elements, 12 bases and 5 aggregates.

That which is not associated with Feeling is included in what? In Feeling, Material existence, Unconditioned and Mind-dissociated impressions; that is to say, 11 elements, 11 bases, and 3 aggregates.

II.4.9. As Feeling paired with Fury is explained, in the same way upto Feeling paired with the rest of the Minor Impure states, Attachment for Immaterial existence, Doubt, five Views, Contact by knowledge and six Groups of Craving are to be explained.

II. 4.10. That which is associated with Feeling, that which is not associated with Attachment for Material existence; (under) 18 elements, 12 bases and 5 aggregates, that which is associated with Feeling is included in what? In Mind-state and Mental state, 8 elements, 2 bases, and 3 aggregates. What is that which is left over? Feeling, Material existence, Unconditioned, and Mind-dissociated impressions; that is to say, 11 elements, 11 bases and 3 aggregates.

That which is not associated with Attachment for Material existence is included in what? In Attachment for Material existence, Material existence, Unconditioned and Mind-dissociated impressions; that is to say, 18 elements, 12 bases and 5 aggregates.

II. 4.11. That which is associated with Attachment for Material existence, that which is not associated with Feeling; (under) 18 elements, 12 bases and 5 aggregates, that which is associated with Attachment for Material existence is included in what? In Mind-state and Mental state, 6 elements, 2 bases and 4 aggregates. What is that which is left over? Attachment for Material existence, Material existence, Unconditioned and Mind-dissociated impressions; that is to say, 18 elements. 12 bases and 5 aggregates.

That which is not associated with Feeling is included in what? In Feeling, Material existence, Unconditioned, and Mind-dissociated impressions; that is to say, 11 elements, 11 bases and 3 aggregates.

II.4.12. That which is associated with Feeling, that which is not associated with Contact by sensorial reaction; (under) 18 elements, 12 bases and 5 aggregates, that which is associated with Feeling is included in what? In Mind-state and Mental state, 8 elements, 2 bases and 3 aggregates. What is that which is left over? Feeling, Material existence, Unconditioned and Mind-dissociated impressions; that is to say, 11 elements, 11 bases and 3 aggregates.

That which is not associated with Contact by sensorial reaction is included in what? In Contact by sensorial reaction, Material existence, Unconditioned and Mind-dissociated impressions; that is to say, 13 elements, 12 bases and 5 aggregates.

II. 4.13. That which is associated with Contact by sensorial reaction, that which is not associated with Feeling; (under) 18 elements, 12 bases and 5 aggregates, that which is associated with Contact by sensorial reaction is included in what? In Mind-state and Mental state, 7 elements, 2 bases and 4 aggregates. What is that which is left over? Contact by sensorial reaction, Material existence, Unconditioned and Mind-dissociated impressions; that is to say, 13 elements, 2 bases and 5 aggregates.

That which is not associated with Feeling is included in what ? In Feeling, Material existence, Unconditioned, and Mind-dissociated impressions; that is to say, 11 elements, 11 bases, and 3 aggregates.

II. 4.14. That which is associated with Feeling, that which is not associated with Verbal Contact; (under) 18 elements, 12 bases and 5 aggregates, that which is associated with Feeling, is included in what ? In Mind-state and Mental state, 8 elements, 2 bases and 3 aggregates. What is that which is left over? Feeling, Material existence, Unconditioned and Mind-dissociated impressions; that is to say, 11 elements, 11 bases and 3 aggregates.

That which is not associated with Verbal Contact is included in what? In Verbal contact, Material existence, Unconditioned, and Mind-dissociated impressions; that is to say, 17 elements, 12 bases and 5 aggregates.

II. 4.15 That which is assoicated with Verbal Contact, that which is not associated with Feeling; (under) 18 elements, 12 bases and 5 aggregates, that which is associated with Verbal Contact is included in what? In Mind-state and Mental state, 3 elements, 2 bases and 4 aggregates. What is that which is left over? Verbal Contact, Material existence, Unconditioned, and Mind-dissociated impressions; that is to say, 17 elements, 12 bases, and 5 aggregates.

That which is not associated with Feeling, is included in what? In Feeling, Material existence, Unconditioned and Mind-dissociated impressions; that is to say, 11 elements, 11 bases, and 3 aggregates.

II. 4.16. That which is associated with Feeling, that which is not associated with Searching state of mind; (under) 18 elements, 12 bases and 5 aggregates, that which is associated with Feeling is included in what? In Mind-state and Mental state, 8 elements, 2 bases, and 3 aggregates. What is that which is left over? Feeling, Material existence, Unconditioned, and Mind-dissociated impressions; that is to say, 11 elements, 11 bases and 3 aggregates.

That which is not associated with Searching state of mind is included in what? In Searching state of mind, Material existence, Unconditioned and Mind-dissociated impressions; that is to say 13 elements, 12 bases and 5 aggregates.

II. 4.17. That which is assoicatd with Searching state of mind, that which is not associated with Feeling; (under) 18 elements, 12 bases and 5 aggregates, that which is associated with Searching stateof mindis included in what? In Mind-state and Mental state, 8 elements, 2 bases and 4 aggregates. What is that which is left over? Searching state of mind, Material existence, Unconditioned, and Mind-dissociated impressions; that is to say, 13 elements, 12 bases and 5 aggregates.

That which is not associated with Feeling is included in what? In Feeling, Material existence, Unconditioned, and Mind-dissociated impressions; that is to say, 11 elements, 11 bases and 3 aggregates.

II. 4.18. As Feeling paired with Searching state of mind is explained, in the same way upto Feeling paired with Investigation are explained.

II. 4.19. That which is associated with Feeling, that which is not associated with Consciousness; (under) 18 elements, 12 bases, and 5 aggregates, that which is associated with Feeling is included in what? In Mind-state and Mental state, 8 elements, 2 bases and 3 aggregates. What is that which is left over? Feeling, Material existence, Unconditioned, and Mind-dissociated impressions; that is to say, 11 elements, 11 bases, and 3 aggregates.

That which is not associated with Consciousness is included in what? In Consciousness, Material existence, Unconditioned, and Mind-dissociated impressions; that is to say, 18 elements, 12 bases and 3 aggregates.

II.4.20. That which is associated with Consciousness, that which is not associated with Feeling; (under) 18 elements, 12 bases, and 5 aggregates, that which is associated with Consciousness, is included in what? In Mental state, 1 element, 1 base, and 3 aggregates. What is that which is left over? Consciousness, Material existence, Unconditioned, and Mind- dissociated impressions; that is to say, 18 elements, 12 bases and 3 aggregates.

That which is not associated with Feeling is included in what? In Feeling, Material existence, Unconditioned, and Mind-dissociated impressions; that is to day, 11 elements. 11 bases and 3 aggregates.

II. 4.21. That which is associated with Feeling, that which is not associated with Eye-consciousness; (under) 18 elements, 12 bases, and 5 aggregates, that which is associated with Feeling is included in what? In Mind-state and Mental state, 8 elements, 2 bases, and 3 aggregates. What is that which is left over? Feeling, Material existence, Unconditioned, and Mind-dissociated impressions; that is to say, 11 elements, 11 bases and 3 aggregates.

That which is not associated with Eye-consciousness is included in what? In Eye-consciousness, Material existence, Unconditioned, and Mind-dissociated impressions; that is to say, 18 elements, 12 bases, and 5 aggregates.

II. 4.22. That which is associated with Eye-consciousness, that which is not associated with Feeling; (under) 18 elements, 12 bases and 5 aggregates, that which is associated with Eye- consciousness is included in what? In Mental state, I element, I base, and 3 aggregates. What is that which is left over? Eye-consciousness, Material existence, Unconditioned, and Mind-dissociated impressions; that is to say, 18 elements, 12 bases and 3 aggregates.

That which is not associated with Feeling is included in what? In Feeling, Material existence, Unconditioned, and Mind-dissociated impressions; that is to say,

11 elements, 11 bases and 3 aggregates.

II.4.23. As Feeling paired with Eye-consciousness is explained, in the same way upto Feeling paired with Mind consciousness are explained.

II.4.24. That which is associated with Feeling, that which is not associated with Visual Contact; (under) 18 elements, 12 bases, and 5 aggregates, that which is associated with Feeling is included in what ? In Mind-state and Mental state, 8 elements, 2 bases, and 3 aggregates. What is that which is left over? Feeling, Material existence, Unconditioned and Mind- dissociated impressions; that is to say, 11 elements, 11 bases and 3 aggregates.

That which is not associated with Visual Contact is included in what ? In Visual Contact, Material existence, Unconditioned, and Mind-dissociated impressions; that is to say, 17 elements, 12 bases, and 5 aggregates.

II.4.25. That which is associated with Visual Contact, that which is not associated with Feeling; (under) 18 elements, 12 bases, and 5 aggregates, that which is associated with Visual Contact is included in what ? In Mental state, 3 elements, 2 bases and 4 aggregates. What is that which is left over ? Visual Contact, Material existence, Unconditioned, and Mind-dissociated impressions; that is to say, 17 elements, 10 bases and 5 aggregates.

That which is not associated with Feeling is included in what? In Feeling, Material existence, Unconditioned, and Mind-dissociated impressions; that is to say, 11 elements, 11 bases, and 3 aggregates.

II.4.26. As Feeling paired with Visual Contact is explained, in the same way upto Feeling paired with Mental Contact are to be explained. As Feeling paired with six Groups of Contact is explained, in the same way upto Feeling paired with six Groups of Notion and Feeling paired with six Groups of Volition are to be explained for details.

5. NOTION AND OTHER STATES

II. 5.1. That which is associated with Notion, that which is not associated with Volition; (under) 18 elements, 12 bases and 5 aggregates, that which is associated with Notion is included in what? In Mind-state and Mental state, 8 elements, 2 bases, and 3 aggregates. What is that which is left over? Notion, Material existence, Unconditioned, and Mind-dissociated impressions; that is to say, 11 elements, 11 bases, and 3 aggregates.

That which is not associated with Volition is included in what ? In Volition, Material existence, Unconditioned, and Mind- dissociated impressions; that is to say, 11 elements, 11 bases, and 2 aggregates.

II.5.2. That which is associated with Volition, that which is not associated with Notion; (under) 18 elements, 12 bases and 5 aggregates, that which is associated with Volition is included in what? In Mind-state and Mental state, 8 elements, 2 bases, and 3 aggregates. What is that which is left over? Volition, Material existence, Unconditioned, and Mind-dissociated impressions; that is to say, 11 elements, 11 bases, and 2 aggregates.

That which is not associated with Notion is included in what? in Notion, Material existence, Unconditioned and Mind-dissociated impressions; that is to say, 11 elements, 11 bases, and 3 aggregates.

II. 5.3. As Notion against Volition is explained, in the same way upto Notion against Discernment is explained.

II. 5.4. That which is associated with Notion, that which is not associated with Unbelief; (under) 18 elements, 12 bases, and 5 aggregates, that which is associated with Notion is included in what ? In Mind-state and Mental state, 8 elements, 2 bases, and 3 aggregates. What is that which is left over ? Notion, Material existence, Unconditioned, and Mind-dissociated impressions; that is to say 11 elements, 11 bases, and 3 aggregates.

That which is not associated with Unbelief is included in what ? In Unbelief, Material existence, Unconditioned, and Mind- dissociated impressions; that is to say, 18 elements, 12 bases and 5 aggregates.

II. 5.5. That which is associated with Unbelief, that which is not associated with Notion; (under) 18 elements, 12 bases, and 5 aggregates, that which is associated with Unbelief is included in what ? In Mind-state and Mental state, 8 elements, 2 bases and 4 aggregates. What is that which is left over ? Unbelief, Material existence, Unconditioned and Mind-dissociated impressions; that is to say, 18 elements, 12 bases, and 5 aggregates.

That which is not associated with Notion, is included in what ? In Notion, Material existence, Unconditioned, and Mind- dissociated impressions; that is to say, 11 elements, 11 bases, and 3 aggregates.

II.5.6. As Notion paired with Volition is explained, in the same way upto the remaining Impure states, Sensuous Attachment, Hatred, Contact by ignorance, Contact by neither knowledge-nor-non-knowledge, Absence of sense of shame, and Absence of fear of blame is explained.

II.5.7. That which is associated with Notion, that which is not associated with Fury; (under) 18 elements, 12 bases, and 5 aggregates, that which is associated with Notion is included in what ? In Mind-state and Mental state, 8 elements, 2 bases, and 3 aggregates. What is that which is left over? Notion, Material existence, Unconditioned, and Mind-dissociated impressions; that is to say, 11 elements, 11 bases, and 3 aggregates.

That which is not associated with Fury is included in what ? In Fury, Material existence, Unconditioned, and Mind-dissociated impressions; that is to say, 18 elements, 12 bases, and 5 aggregates.

II.5.8. That which is associated with Fury, that which is not associated with Notion; (under) 18 elements, 12 bases and 5 aggregates, that which is associated with Fury, is included in what ? In Mind-state and Mental state, 3 elements, 2 bases, and 4 aggregates. What is that which is left over ? Fury, Material existence, Unconditioned, and Mind-dissociated impressions; that is to say, 11 elements, 11 bases; and 3 aggregates.

That which is not associated with Notion is included in what ? In Notion, Material existence, Unconditioned, and Mind-dissociated impressions; that is to say, 11 elements, 11 bases, and 3 aggregates.

II. 5.9. As Notion paired with Fury is explained, in the same way, upto Notion paired with the remaining Minor Impure states, Attachment for Immaterial existence,

Doubt, five Views, Contact by knowledge, and Six Groups of Craving are to be explained.

II. 5.10. That which is associated with Notion, that which is not associated with Sensuous Attachment; (under) 18 elements, 12 bases and 5 aggregates, that which is associated with Notion, is included in what ? In Mind-state and Mental state, 8 elements, 2 bases and 3 aggregates. What is that which is left over? Notion, Material existence, Unconditioned, and Mind- dissociated impressions; that is to say, 11 elements, 11 bases, and 3 aggregates.

That which is not associated with Sensuous Attachment is included in what? In Attachment, Material existence, Unconditioned, and Mind-dissociated impressions; that is to say, 18 elements, 12 bases, and 5 aggregates.

II.5.11. That which is associated with Sensuous Attachment, that which is not associated with Notion; (under) 18 elements, 12 bases, and 5 aggregates, that which is associated with Sensuous Attachment is included in what? In Mind- state and Mental state, 6 elements, 2 bases, and 4 aggregates. What is that which is left over ? Sensuous Attachment, Material Existence, Unconditioned and Mind-dissociated impressions; that is to say, 18 .elements, 12 bases and 5 aggregates.

That which is not associated with Notion is included in what ? In Notion, Material Existence, Unconditioned, and Mind-dissociated impressions; that is to say 11 elements, 11 bases and 3 aggregates.

II.5.12. That which is associated with Notion, that which is not associated with Contact by sensorial reaction; (under) 18 elements, 12 bases and 5 aggregates, that which is associated with Notion is included in what? In Mind-state and Mental state, 8 elements, 2 bases, and 3 aggregates. What is that which is left over? Notion, Material existence,

Unconditioned and Mind-dissociated impressions; that is to say 11 elements, 11 bases, and 3 aggregates.

That which is not associated with Contact by sensorial reaction is included in what ? In Contact by sensorial reaction, Material existence, Unconditioned, and Mind-dissociated impressions; that is to say, 13 elements, 12 bases and 5 aggregates.

II. 5.13. That which is associated with Contact by sensorial reaction, that which is not associated with Notion; (under) 18 elements, 12 bases and 5 aggregates, that which is associated with Contact by sensorial reaction is included in what? In Mind-state and Mental state, 7 elements, 2 bases, and 4 aggregates. What is that which is left over? Contact by sensorial reaction, Material existence, Unconditioned, and Mind-dissociated impressions; that is to say, 13 elements, 12 bases, and 5 aggregates.

That which is not associated with Notion is included in what? In Notion, Material existence, Unconditioned, and Mind-dissociated impressions; that is to say, 11 elements, 11 bases, and 3 aggregates.

II. 5.14. That which is associated with Notion, that which is not associated with Verbal Contact; (under) 18 elements, 12 bases, and 5 aggregate, that which is associated with Notion is included in what? In Mind-state and Mental state, 8 elements, 2 bases, and 3 aggregates. What is that which is left over? Notion, Material existence, Unconditioned and Mind-dissociated impressions; that is to say, 11 elements, 11 bases and 3 aggregates.

That which is not associated with Verbal Contact is included in what? In Verbal Contact, Material existence, Unconditioned, and Mind-dissociated impressions; that is to say, 17 elements, 12 bases, and 5 aggregates.

II.5.15. That which is associated with Verbal contact, that which is not associated with Notion; (Under), 18 elements

12 bases, and 5 aggregates, that which is associated with Verbal Contact is included in what ? In Mind-state and Mental state, 3 elements, 2 bases and 4 aggregates. What is that which is left over? Verbal Contact, Material existence, Unconditioned, and Mind-dissociated impressions; that is to say, 17 elements, 12 bases, and 5 aggregates.

That which is not associated with Notion is included in what ? In Notion, Material existence, Unconditioned, and Mind- dissociated impressions; that is to say, 11 elements, 11 bases, and 3 aggregates.

II. 5.16. That which is associated with Notion, that which is not associated with Faculty for feeling pleasure; (under) 18 elements, 12 bases, and 5 aggregates, that which is associated with Notion is included in what ? In Mind-state and Mental state, 8 elements, 2 bases, and 3 aggregates. What is that which is left over? Notion, Material existence, Unconditioned, and Mind-dissociated impressions; that is to say, 11 elements, 11 bases and 3 aggregates.

That which is not associated with Faculty for feeling of pleasure, is included in what ? In Faculty for feeling pleasure, Material existence, Unconditioned, and Mind-dissociated impression; that is to say, 18 elements, 12 bases and 5 aggregates.

II.5.17. That which is associated with Faculty for feeling pleasure, that which is not associated with Notion; (under) 18 elements, 12 bases, and 5 aggregates, that which is associated with Faculty feeling pleasure is included in what ? In Mind-state and Mental state, 8 elements, 2 bases and 3 aggregates. What is that which is left over? Faculty for pleasure, Material existence, Unconditioned, and Mind-dissociated impressions; that is to say, 18 elements, 12 bases, and 5 aggregates.

That which is not associated with Notion is included in what ? In Notion, Material existence, Unconditioned, and Mind-dissociated impressions; that is to say, 11 elements, 11 bases, and 3 aggregates.

II. 5.18. As Notion paired with Faculty for feeling pleasure is explained, in the same way Notion paired with Faculty for feeling indifference is to be explained.

II. 5.19. That which is associated with Notion, that which is not associated with Faculty for feeling pain; (under) 18 elements, 12 bases and 5 aggregates, that which is associated with Notion is included in what? In Mind-state and Mental state, 8 elements, 2 bases, and 3 aggregates. What is that which is left over? Notion, Material existence, Unconditioned, and Mind-dissociated impressions; that is to say, 11 elements, 11 bases, and 5 aggregates.

That which is not associated with Faculty for feeling pain is included in what ? In Faculty for feeling pain, Material existence, Unconditioned, and Mind-dissociated impressions; that is to say, 18 elements, 12 bases and 5 aggregates.

II.5.20. That which is associated with Faculty for feeling pain, that which is not associated with Notion; (under) 18 elements, 12 bases and 5 aggregates, that which is associated with Faculty for feeling pain is included in what? In Mind-state and Mental state, 7 elements, 2 bases, and 3 aggregates. What is that which is left over? Faculty for feeling pain, Material existence, Unconditioned and Mind-dissociated impressions; that is to say, 18 elements, 12 bases, and 5 aggregates.

That which is not associated with Notion is included in what? In Notion, Material existence, Unconditioned, and Mind-dissociated impressions; that is to say, 11 elements 11 bases, and 3 aggregates.

II.5.21. That which is associated with Notion, that which is not associated with Faculty for feeling of satisfaction; (under) 18 elements, 12 bases and 5 aggregates, that which is associated with Notion is included in what? In Mind-state and Mental state, 8 elements, 2 bases, and 3 aggregates. What is that which left over? Notion, Material existence, Unconditioned, and Mind-dissociated impressions; that is to say, 11 elements, 11 bases and 3 aggregates.

That which is not associated with Faculty for feeling satisfaction is included in what? In Faculty for feeling satisfaction, Material existence, Unconditioned, and Mind-dissociated impressions; that is to say, 18 elements, 12 bases and 5 aggregates.

II. 5.22. That which is associated with Faculty for feeling satisfaction, that which is not associated with Notion, (under) 18 elements, 12 bases and 5 aggregates that which is associated with Faculty for feeling satisfaction is included in what? In Mind-state and Mental state, 3 elements, 2 bases, and 3 aggregates. What is that which is left over? Faculty for satisfaction, Material existence, Unconditioned and Mind-dissociated impressions; that is to say, 18 elements, 12 bases, and 5 aggregates.

That which is not associated with Notion is included in what? In Notion, Material existence, Unconditioned and Mind-dissociated impressions; that is to say, 11 elements, 11 bases and 3 aggregates.

II.5.23. As Notion paired with Faculty for feeling satisfaction is explained, in the same way Notion paired with Faculty for feeling dissatisfaction is to be explained.

II.5.24. Notion paired with Searching state of mind, Investigation, Consciousness, six Groups of Consciousness, six Groups of Contact, and six Groups of Volition - all are to be explained like it is explained in the category of Feeling. Only in place of Feeling, it should be mentioned as Notion.

II. 5.25 That which is associated with Notion, that which is not associated with Feeling born of Visual Contact; (under) 18 elements, 12 bases, and 5 aggregates, that which is associated with Notion in included in what? In Mind-state and Mental state, 8 elements, 2 bases, and 3 aggregates. What is that which is left over? Notion, Material existence, Unconditioned, and Mind-dissociated impressions; that is to say, 11 elements, 11 bases and 3 aggregates.

That which is not associated with Feeling born of Visual Contact is included in what? In Visual Contact, Material existence, Unconditioned, and Mind-dissociated impressions; that is to say, 17 elements, 12 bases, and 5 aggregates.

II.5.26. That which is associated with Feeling born of Visual Contact, that which is not associated with Notion; (under) 18 elements, 12 bases and 5 aggregates, that which is associated with Feeling born of Visual Contact is included in what? In Mind-state and Mental state, 3 elements, 2 bases, and 3 aggregates. What is that which is left over? Feeling born of Visual Contact, Material existence, Unconditioned, and Mind-dissociated impressions; that is to say, 17 elements, 12 bases, and 5 aggregates.

That which is not associated with Notion is included in what? In Notion, Material existence, Unconditioned, and Mind-dissociated impressions; that is to say, 11 elements, 11 bases, and 3 aggregates.

II.5.27. As Notion paired with Feeling born of visual contact is explained, in the same way upto Notion paired with Feeling born of mental contact is to be explained.

6. VOLITION AND OTHER STATES

II. 6.1. That which is associated with Volition, that which is not associated with Contact; (under) 18 elements, 12 bases and 5 aggregates, that which is associated with Volition is included in what? In Mind-state and Mental state, 8 elements, 2 bases and 4 aggregates. What is that which is left over? Volition, Material existence, Unconditioned and Mind-dissociated impressions; that is to say, 11 elements, 11 bases, and 2 aggregates.

That which is not associated with Contact is included in what? In Contact, Material existence, Unconditioned and Mind- dissociated impressions; that is to say, 11 elements, 11 bases and 2 aggregates.

II.6.2. That which is associated with Contact, that which is not associated with Volition; (under) 18 elements, 12 bases and 5 aggregates, that which is associated with Contact is included in what? In Mind-state and Mental state, 8 elements, 2 bases, and 4 aggregates. What is that which is left over? Contact, Material existence, Unconditioned and Mind-dissociated impressions; that is to say, 11 elements, 11 bases, and 2 aggregates. That which is not associated with Volition is included in what? In Volition, Material existence, Unconditioned and Mind-dissociated impressions; that is to say, 11 elements, 11 bases, and 2 aggregates.

II.6.3. As Volition paired with Contact is explained, in the same way upto Volition paired with Discernment are explained.

II.6.4. That which is associated with Volition, that which is not associated with Unbelief; (under) 18 elements, 12 bases, and 5 aggregates, that which is associated with Volition is included in what? In Mind-state and Mental state, 8 elements, 2 bases, and 4 aggregates. What is that which is left over? Volition, Material existence, Unconditioned, and Mind-dissociated impressions; that is to say, 11 elements, 11 bases, and 2 aggregates.

That which is not associated with Unbelief is included in what? In Unbelief, Material existence, Unconditioned, and Mind- dissociated impressions; that is to say, 18 elements, 12 bases and 5 aggregates.

II. 6.5. That which is associated with Unbelief, that which is not associated with Volition; (under) 18 elements, 12 bases and 5 aggregates, that which is associated with Unbelief is included in what ? In Mind-state and Mental state, 8 elements, 2 bases, and 4 aggregates. What is that which is left over? Unbelief, Material existence, Unconditioned, and Mind-dissociated impressions; that is to say, 18 elements, 12 bases and 5 aggregates.

That which is not associated with Volition is included in what? In Volition, Material existence, Unconditioned, and Mind-dissociated impressions; that is to say, 11 elements, 11 bases, and 2 aggregates.

II. 6.6. As Notion paired with Unbelief is explained, in the same way Notion paired with Impure states, Sensuous Attachment, Hatred, Contact by ignorance, and Contact by neither-knowledge-nor-non-knowledge, are to be explained.

II.6.7. That which is associated with Notion, that which is not associated with Fury; (under) 18 elements, 12 bases, and 5 aggregates, that which is associated with Notion is included in what? In Mind-state and Mental state, 8 elements, 2 bases, and 4 aggregates. What is that which is left over? Notion, Material existence, Unconditioned, and Mind-dissociated impressions; that is to say, 11 elements, 11 bases, and 2 aggregates.

That which is not associated with Fury is included in what? In Fury, Material existence, Unconditioned, and

Mind-dissociated impressions, that is to say, 18 elements, 12 bases, and 5 aggregates.

II. 6.8. That which is associated with Fury, that which is not associated with Volition; (under) 18 elements, 12 bases, and 5 aggregates, that which is associated with Fury is included in what ? In Mind-state and Mental state, 3 elements, 2 bases, and 4 aggregates. What is that which is left over? Fury, Material existence, Unconditioned, and Mind-dissociated impressions; that is to say, 18 elements, 12 bases, and 5 aggregates.

That which is not associated with Volition is included. in what? In Volition, Material existence, Unconditioned and Mind- dissociated impressions, that is to say 11 elements, 11 bases, and 2 aggregates.

II.6.9. As Volition paired with Fury is explained, in the same way Volition paired with remaining Minor Impure state, Attachment for Immaterial existence, Doubt, five Views, Contact by knowledge, six Groups of Craving are to be explained.

II. 6.10. That which is associated with Volition, that which is not associated with Attachment for Material existence; (under) 18 elements, 12 bases and 5 aggregates, that which is associated with Volition is included in what? In Mind-state and Mental state, 8 elements, 2 bases, and 4 aggregates. What is that which is left over? Volition, Material existence, Unconditioned, and Mind-dissociated impressions; that is to say, 11 elements, 11 bases, and 2 aggregates.

That which is not associated with Attachment for Material existence is included in what? In Attachment for Material existence, Material existence, Unconditioned, and Mind-dissociated impressions, that is to say 18 elements, 12 bases, and 5 aggregates.

II.6.11. That which is associated with Attachment for Material existence, that which is not associated with Volition; (under) 18 elements,. 12 bases, and 5 aggregates, that which is associated with Attachment for Material existence is included in what? In Mind-state and Mental state, 6 elements,2 bases, and 4 aggregates. What is that which is left over ? Attachment for Material existence, Material existence, Unconditioned, and Mind-dissociated impressions; that is to say, 18 elements, 12 bases, and 5 aggregates.

That which is not associated with Volition is included in what ? In Volition, Material existence, Unconditioned, and Mind- dissociated impressions, that is to say, 11 elements, 11 bases, and 2 aggregates.

II. 6.12. That which is associated with Volition, that which is not associated with Contact by sensorial reaction; (under) 18 elements, 12 bases, and 5 aggregates, that which is associated with Volition is included in what? In Mind-state and Mental state, 8 elements, 2 bases, and 4 aggregates. What is that is left over? Volition, Material existence, Unconditioned, and Mind-dissociated impressions; that is to say, 11 elements, 11 bases, and 2 aggregates.

That which is not associated with Contact by sensorial reaction is included in what? In Contact by sensorial reaction, Material existence, Unconditioned and Mind-dissociated impressions; that is to say, 13 elements, 2 bases and 5 aggregates.

II. 6.13. That which is associated with Contact by sensorial reaction, that which is not associated with Volition; (under) 18 elements, 12 bases, and 5 aggregates, that which is associated with Contact by sensorial reaction is included in what? In Mind-state and Mental state, 7 elements, 2 bases, and 4 aggregates are to be explained.

What is that which is left over? Contact by sensorial reaction, Material existence, Unconditioned, and Mind-dissociated impressions; that is to say, 13 elements, 12 bases and 5 aggregates.

That which is not associated with Volition is included in what? In Volition, Material existence, Unconditioned and Mind-dissociated impressions; that is to say, 11 elements, 11 bases and 2 aggregates.

II. 6.14. That which is associated with Volition, that which is not associated with Verbal Contact; (under) 18 elements, 12 bases, and 5 aggregates, that which is associated with Volition is to be explained as explained before. That which is not associated with Verbal Contact is to be explained as explained before, but with regard to 5 aggregates, it should be 2 aggregates. Like that which is associated with Volition is explained, in the same way that which is not associated with Verbal Contact is to be explained.

II. 6.15. That which is associated with Verbal Contact, that which is not associated with Notion-should be explained in the manner already explained before.

II. 6.16. That which is associated with Volition, that which is not associated with Faculty for satisfaction; that which is associated with Faculty for satisfaction, that which is not associated with Volition are to be explained in the manner already mentioned.

II. 6.17. As Volition paired with Faculty for satisfaction is explained, in the same way Volition paired with Faculty for dissatisfaction is to be explained.

II.6.18. Volition paired with Searching state of mind Investigation, Consciousness, six Groups of Consciousness, Six Groups of Contact, six Groups of Feeling and six Groups of Notion are to be calculated following what is said before.

At the end of *chüan* II it is said : the *Dhātukāyapādaśāstra* belongs to the *Sarvāstivāda* school.

7. CONTACT AND OTHER STATES

II. 7.1. That which is associated with Contact, that which is not associated with Attention; (under) 18 elements, 12 bases, and 5 aggregates, that which is associated with Contact is to be explained like before, but with regard to 5 aggregates, it should be 2 aggregates.

That which is not associated with Attention is included in what? In Attention, Material existence, Unconditioned, Mind-dissociated impressions; that is to say, 11 elements, 11 bases and 2 aggregates.

II.7.2. That which is associated with Attention, that which is not associated with Contact; (under) 18 elements, 12 bases, and 5 aggregates, that which is associated with Attention is included in what? In Attention, Mind-state and Mental state, 8 elements, 2 bases, and 4 aggregates. What is that which is left over? Attention, Material existence, Unconditioned and Mind-dissociated impressions; that is to say, 11 elements, 11 bases and 2 aggregates.

That which is not associated with Contact etc. is to be explained in the same way it has been explained before.

II.7.3. As Contact paired with Attention is explained, in the same way upto Contact paired with Discernment are to be explained.

II.7.4. That which is associated with Contact, that which is not assoicatd with Unbelief; that which is associated with Unbelief, that which is not associated with Contact-these are to be explained in the manner already mentioned before.

II. 7.5. As Contact paired with Unbelief is explained, in the same way Contact paired with the remaining Impure states, Sensuous Attachment, Hatred, Absence of sense of shame and Absence of fear of blame are to be explained.

II. 7.6. That which is associated with Contact, that which is not associated with Fury; that which is associated with Fury, that which is not associated with Contact-these are to be explained in the manner already mentioned before.

II.7.7. As Contact paired with Fury is explained, in the same way Contact paired with the remaining Minor Impure states, Attachment for Immaterial existence, Doubt, five Views, six Groups of Craving are to be explained.

II. 7.8. That which is associated with Contact, that which is not ássociated with Attachment for Material existence that which is associatéd with Attachment for Material existence, that which is not associated with Contact-these are to be explained in the manner already mentioned before.

II. 7.9. That which is associated with Contact, that which is not associated with Faculty for pleasure; that which is associated with Faculty for pleasure, that which is not associated with Contact -these are to be explained in the manner already mentioned before.

II. 7.10. As Contact paired with Faculty for pleasure is explained, in the same way Contact paired with Faculty for indifference is to be explained.

II. 7.11. That which is associated with Contact, that which is not associated with Faculty for pain; that which is associated with Faculty for pain, that which is not associated with Contact are to be explained in the manner already mentioned before.

II. 7.12. That which is associated with Contact, that which is not associated with Faculty for satisfaction; that which is associated with Faculty for satisfaction, that which is not associated with Contact - these are to be explained in the manner already mentioned before.

II. 7.13. As Contact paired with Faculty for satisfaction is explained, in the same way Contact paired with Craving is also explained.

II. 7.14. Contact paired with Searching state of mind Investigation, Consciousness, six Groups of Consciousness, six Groups of Feeling, six Groups of Notion, six Groups of Volition are to be explained in the manner already mentioned before.

8. ATTENTION AND OTHER STATES

II. 8.1. That which is associated with Attention, that which is not associated with Desire; (under) 18 elements, 12 bases and 5aggregates, that which is associated etc. is to be explained as before.

That which is not associated with Desire is included in what? In Desire, Material existence, Unconditioned and Mind-dissociated impressions; that is to say, 11 elements, 11 bases, and 2 aggregates.

II. 8.2. That which is associated with Desire, that which is not associated with Attention; (under) 18 elements, 12 bases and 5 aggregates, that which is associated with Desire is included in what ? In Mind-state and Mental state, 8 elements, 2 bases and 4 aggregates. What is that which is left over? Desire, Material existence, Unconditioned and Mind-dissociated impressions; That is to say, 11 elements, 11 bases, and 2 aggregates.

That which is not associated with Attention etc. is to be explained as before.

II. 8.3. As Attention paired with Desire is explained, in the same way upto Attention paired with Discernment is to be explained.

II. 8.4. That which is associated with Attention, that which is not associated with Unbelief; that which is associated with Unbelief, that which is not associated with Attention-these are to be explained in the manner already mentioned before.

II. 8.5. As Attention paired with Unbelief is explained, in the same way Attention paired with remaining Impure states, Sensuous Attachment, Hatred, Contact by ignorance, Contact by neither-knowledge-nor-non-knowledge, Absence of sense of shame, and Absence of sense of fear are to be explained.

II. 8.6. That which is associated with Attention, that which is not associated with Fury; that which is associated with Fury, that which is not associated with Attention-these are to be explained in the manner already mentioned before.

II.8.7. As Attention paired with Fury is explained, in the same way Attention paired with the remaining Impure states, Attachment for Immaterial existence, Doubt, five Views, Contact by Knowledge, six Groups of Craving are to be explained,

II. 8.8. That which is associated with Attention, that which is not associated with Contact by sensorial reaction; that which is associated with Contact by sensorial reaction, that which is not associated with Attention-these are to be explained in the manner already mentioned before.

II. 8.9. That which is associated with Attention, that which is not associated with Verbal Contact; that which is associated with Verbal Contact, that which is not associated with Attention-these are to be explained in the manner already mentioned before.

II. 8.10. That which is associated with Attention, that which is not associated with Faculty for pleasure; that which is associated with Faculty for pleasure, that which is not associated with Attention-these are to be explained in the manner already mentioned before.

II.8.11. As Attention paired with Faculty for pleasure is explained , in the same way Attention paired with Faculty for indifference is to be explained.

II. 8.12. That which is associated with Attention, that which is not associated with Faculty for pain; that which is associated with Faculty for pain, that which is not associated with Attention-these are to be explained in the manner already mentioned before.

II. 8.13. That which is associated with Attention, that which is not associated with Faculty for satisfaction; that which is associated with Faculty for satisfaction, that which is not associated with Attention-these are to be explained in the manner already mentioned before.

II. 8.14. As Attention paired with faculty for satisfaction is explained, in the same way Attention paired with Faculty for dissatisfaction is to be explained.

II. 8.15. Attention paired with Searching state of mind Investigation, Consciousness, six Groups of Consciousness, six Groups of Contact, six Groups of Feeling, six Groups of Notion are to be explained in the manner already mentioned before.

9. DESIRE AND OTHER STATES

II. 9.1. That which is associated with Desire, that which is not associated with Approbation; (under) 18 elements, 12 bases, and 5 aggregates, that which is associated with Desire etc. is to be explained as before.

That which is not associated with Approbation is included in what ? In Approbation, Material existence, Unconditioned, and Mind- dissociated impressions; that is to say, 11 elements, 11 bases, and 5 aggregates.

II. 9.2. That which is associated with Approbation, that which is not associated with Desire; (under) 18 elements, 12 bases and 5 aggregates, that which is associated with Approbation is included in what? In Mind-state and Mental state, 8 elements, 2 bases, and 4 aggregates. What is that which is left over? Approbation, Material existence, Unconditioned, and Mind- dissociated impressions; that is to say, 11 elements, 11 bases, and 2 aggregates.

That which is not associated with Desire etc. is to be explained as before.

II. 9.3. As Desire paired with Approbation is explained, in the same way Desire paired with Memory, Concentration, and Discernment are to be explained.

II. 9.4. That which is associated with Desire, that which is not associated with Unbelief; that which is associated with Unbelief, that which is not associated with Desire these are to be explained in the manner as already mentioned before.

II. 9.5. As Desire paired with Unbelief is explained, in the same way Desire paired with the remaining Impure states, Sensuous Attachment, Hatred, Contact by ignorance, Contact by neither-knowledge-nor-non-knowledge, Absence of sense of shame, Absence of sense of fear are to be explained.

II. 9.6. That which is assoicatd with Desire, that which is not associated with Fury; that which is associated with Fury, that which is not associated with Desire-these are to be explained in the manner as already mentioned before.

II. 9.7. As Desire paired with Fury is explained, in the same way Desire paired with remaining Minor Impure state, Attachment for Immaterial existence, Hatred, five Views, Contact by knowledge, six Groups of Craving are to be explained.

II. 9.8 That which is associated with Desire, that which is not associated with Attachment for Material existence; that which is associated with Attachment for Material existence, that which is not associated with Desire-these are to be explained in the manner as already mentioned before.

II. 9.9. That which is associated with Desire, that which is not associated with Contact by sensorial reaction; that which is associated with Contact by sensorial reaction, that which is not associated with Desire-these are to be explained in the manner already mentioned before.

II. 9.10. That which is associated with Desire, that which is not associated with Verbal Contact; that which is associated with Verbal Contact, that which is not associated with Desire-these are to be explained in the manner already mentioned before.

II. 9.11. That which is associated with Desire, that which is not associated with Faculty for pleasure; that which is associated with Faculty for pleasure, that which is not associated with Desire-these are to be explained in the manner already mentioned before.

II.9.12. As Desire paired with Faculty for pleasure is explained, in the same way Desire paired with Faculty for indifference is to be explained.

II. 9.13. That which is associated with Desire, that which is not associated with Faculty for pain; that which is associated with Faculty for pain, that which is not associated with Desire-these are to be explained in the manner already mentioned before.

II. 9.14. That which is associated with Desire, that which is not associated with Faculty for satisfaction; that which is associated with Faculty for satisfaction, that which is not associated with Desire-these are to be explained in the manner already mentioned before.

II. 9.15. As Desire paired with Faculty for satisfaction is explained, in the same way Desire paired with Faculty for dissatisfaction is to be explained.

II. 9.16. Desire paired with Searching state of mind Investigation, Consciousness, six Groups of Contact, six Groups of Feeling, six Groups of Notion, six Groups of Volition are to be explained in the manner already mentioned before.

10. APPROBATION AND OTHER STATES

II. 10.1. That which is associated with Approbation, that which is not associated with Memory; (under) 18 elements, 12 bases, and 5 aggregates, that which is associated with etc. is to be explained as before.

That which is not associated with Memory is included in what? In Memory, Material existence, Unconditioned, and Mind-dissociated impressions, that is to say, 11 elements, 11 bases, and 2 aggregates.

II. 10.2. That which is associated with Memory, that which is not associated with Approbation; (under) 18 elements, 12 bases and 5 aggregates, that which is associated with Memory is included in what ? In Mind-state and Mental state, 8 elements, 2 bases and 4 aggregates. What is that which is left over? Memory, Material existence, Unconditioned and Mind-dissociated impressions, that is to say, 11 elements, 11 bases, and 2 aggregates.

That which is not associated with Approbation is to be explained as before.

II. 10.3. As Approbation paired with Memory is explained, in the same way Approbation paired with Concentration and Discernment are to be explained.

II. 10.4. That which is associated with Approbation, that which is not associated with Unbelief; that which is associated with Unbelief, not associated with Approbation-these are to be explained in the manner as already mentioned before.

II. 10.5. As Approbation paired with Memory is explained, in the same way Approbation paired with the remaining Impure states, Sensuous Attachment, Hatred, Contact by ignorance, Contact by neither-knowledge-nor-non-knowledge, Absence of sense of shame, Absence of sense of fear are to be explained.

II.10.6. That which is associated with Approbation, that which is not associated with Fury; that which is associated with Fury, that which is not associated with Approbation-these are to be explained in the manner as already mentioned before.

II. 10.7. As Approbation paired with Fury is explained, in the same way Approbation paired with Minor Impure states, Attachment for Immaterial existence, Hatred, five Views, Contact by knowledge, six Groups of Craving are to be explained.

II. 10.8. That which is associated with Approbation, that which is not associated with Attachment for Material existence; that which is associated with Attachment for Material existence, that which is not associated with Approbation-these are to be explained in the manner as already mentioned earlier.

II. 10.9 That which is associated with Approbation, that which is not associated with Contact by sensorial reaction; that which is associated with Contact by sensorial reaction, that which is not associated with Approbation-these are to explained in the manner as mentioned earlier.

II. 10.11 That which is associated with Approbation, that which is not associated with Faculty for pleasure; that which is associated with Faculty for pleasure, that which not associated with Approbation-these are to be explained in the manner as mentioned earlier.

II. 10.12. As Approbation paired with Faculty for pleasure is explained, in the same way Approbation paired with Faculty for indifference is to be explained.

II. 10.13. That which is associated with Approbation, that which is not associated with Faculty for pain; that which is assoicated with Faculty for pain, that which is not associated with Approbation-these are to be explained following the calculation as mentioned earlier.

II. 10.14. That which is associated with Approbation, that which is not associated with Faculty for satisfaction; that which is associated with Faculty for satisfaction, that which is not associated with Approbation-these are to be explained following the calculation as mentioned earlier.

II. 10.15. As Approbation paired with Faculty for satisfaction is explained, in the same way Approbation paired with Faculty for dissatisfaction is to be explained.

II. 10.16. Approbation paired with Searching state of mind Investigation, Consciousness, six Groups of Consciousness, six Groups of Contact, six Groups of Feeling, six Groups of Notion, six Groups of Volition are to be explained following the calculation as mentioned earlier.

11. MEMORY AND OTHER STATES

II. 11.1. That which is associated with Memory, that which is not associated with Concentration; (under) 18 elements, 12 bases, and 5 aggregates, that which is associated with Concentration etc. is to be explained in the same way as mentioned earlier.

That which is associated with Concentration is included in what? In Concentration, Material existence, Unconditioned, and Mind-dissociated impressions; that is to say 11 elements, 11 bases, and 2 aggregates.

II. 11.2. That which is associated with Concentration, that which is not associated with Memory; (under) 18 elements,

12 bases, and 5 aggregates, that which is associated with Concentration is included in what? In Mind-state and Mental state, 8 elements, 2 bases and 4 aggregates. What is that which is left over? Concentration, Material existence, Unconditioned, and Mind-dissociated impressions, that is to say, 11 elements, 11 bases and 2 aggregates.

That which is not associated with Memory etc. is to be explained in the same way as mentioned earlier.

II. 11.3. As Memory paired with Concentration is explained, in the same way Memory paired with Discernment is to be explained.

II. 11.4. That which is associated with Memory, that which is not associated with Unbelief; that which is associated with Unbelief, that which is not associated with Memory-these are to be explained following the calculation as mentioned earlier.

II.11.5. As Memory paired with Unbelief is explained, in the same way Memory paired with the remaining Impure states, Sensuous Attachment, Hatred, Contact by Ignorance, Contact by neither-knowledge-nor-non-knowledge, Absence of sense of shame, Absence of sense of fear, are to be explained.

II. 11.6. That which is associated with Memory, that which is not associated with Fury; That which is associated with Fury, that which is not associated with Memory-these are to be explained following the calculation as mentioned above.

II. 11.7. As Memory paired with Fury is explained, in the same way Memory paired with the remaining Minor Impure states, Attachment for Immaterial existence, Doubt, five Views, Contact by Knowledge, six Groups of Craving are to be explained.

II. 11.8. That which is associated with Memory, that which is not associated with Attachment for Material existence; that which is associated with Attachment for Material existence, that which is not associated with Memory-these are to be explained following the calculation as mentioned earlier.

II. 11.9. That which is associated with Memory, that which is not associated with Contact by sensorial reaction; that which is associated with Contact by sensorial reaction, that which is not associated with Memory-these are to be explained following the calculation as mentioned earlier.

II. 11.10. That which is associated with Memory, that which is not associated with Verbal Contact; that which is associated with Verbal Contact, that which is not associated with Memory-these are to be explained following the calculation as mentioned earlier.

II.11.11. That which is associated with Memory, that which is not associated with Faculty for satisfaction; that which is associated with Faculty for satisfaction, that which is not associated with Memory-these are to be explained following the calculation as mentioned earlier.

II. 11.12. As Memory paired with Faculty for satisfaction is explained, in the same way Memory paired with Faculty for indifference is to be explained.

II.11.13. That which is associated with Memory, that which is not associated with Faculty for pain; that which is associated with Faculty for pain, that which is not associated with Memory-these are to be explained following the calculation as mentioned earlier.

II. 11.14. That which is associated with Memory, that which is not associated with Faculty for satisfaction; that which is associated with Faculty for satisfaction, that which is not associated with Memory-these are to be explained following the calculation as mentioned earlier.

II. 11.15. As Memory paired with Faculty for satisfaction is explained, in the same way Memory against Faculty for dissatisfaction is to be explained.

II. 11.16. Memory paired with Searching state of mind Investigation, Consciousness, six Groups of Contact, six Groups of Feeling, six Groups of Notion, six Groups of Volition are to be explained following the calculation as mentioned earlier.

12. CONCENTRATION AND OTHER STATES

II. 12.1. That which is associated with Concentration, that which is not associated with Discernment; (under) 18 elements, 12 bases and 5 aggregates, that which is associated with Concentration is included in what? In Mind-state and Mental state, 11 elements, 11 bases, and 2 aggregates. What is that which is left over? It is to be explained in the way as explained earlier.

That which is not associated with Discernment is included in what? In Discernment, Material existence, Unconditioned, and Mind-dissociated impressions, that is to say, 11 elements, 11 bases and 2 aggregates.

II. 12.2. That which is associated with Discernment, that which is not associated with Concentration; (under) 18 elements, 12 bases, and 5 aggregates, that which is associated with Discernment is included in what ? In Mind-state and Mental state, 8 elements 2 bases and 4 aggregates. What is that which is left over? Discernment, Material existence, Unconditioned, and Mind-dissociated impressions. That is to say, 11 elements, 11 bases and 2 aggregates. That which is associated with Concentration etc. is to be explained in the way as explained earlier.

II. 12.3. That which is associated with Concentration, that which is not associated with Unbelief; that which is associated with Unbelief, that which is not associated with

Concentration-these are to be explained following the calculation as mentioned earlier.

II.12.4. As Concentration paired with Unbelief is explained, in the same way Concentration against the remaining Impure states, Sensuous Attachment, Hatred, Contact by ignorance, Contact by neither-knowledge-nor-non-knowledge, Absence of sense of shame, Absence of sense of fear are to be explained.

II.12.5. That which is associated with Concentration, that which is not associated with Fury; that which is associated with Fury, that which is not associated with Concentration-these are to be explained following the calculation as mentioned earlier.

II.12.6. As Concentration paired with Fury is explained, in the same way Concentration paired with Minor Impure states, Attachment for Immaterial existence, Doubt, Five Views, Contact by knowledge, Six Groups of Craving are to be explained.

II. 12.7. That which is associated with Concentration, that which is not associated with Attachment for Material existence; that which is associated with Attachment for Materiel existence, that which is not associated with Concentration-these are to be explained following the calculation as mentioned earlier.

II. 12.8. That which is associated with Concentration, that which is not associated with Contact by sensorial reaction; that which is associated with Contact by sensorial reaction, that which is not associated with Concentration-these are to be explained following the calculation as mentioned earlier.

II. 12.9. That which is associated with Concentration, that which is not associated with Verbal Contact; that which is associated with Verbal Contact, that which is not associated with Concentration-these are to be explained following the calculation as mentioned earlier.

II. 12.10. That which is associated with Concentration, that which is not associated with Faculty for pleasure, that which is associated with Faculty for pleasure, that which is not associated with Concentration-these are to be explained following the calculation as mentioned earlier.

II. 12.11. As Concentration paired with Faculty for pleasure is explained, in the same way Concentration paired with Faculty for indifference is to be explained.

II. 12.12 That which is associated with Concentration, that which is not associated with Faculty for pain; that which is associated with Faculty for pain, that which is not associated with Concentration-these are to be explained following the calculation as mentioned earlier.

II. 12.13. That which is associated with Concentration, that which is not associated with Faculty for satisfaction; that which is associated with Faculty for satisfaction, that which is not associated with Concentration-these are to be explained following the calculation as mentioned earlier.

II. 12.14. As Concentration paired with Faculty for satisfaction is explained, in the same way Concentration paired with Faculty for dissatisfaction is to be explained.

II. 12.15. Concentration paired with Searching state of mind Investigation, Consciousness, six Groups of Consciousness, six Groups of Contact, six Groups of Feeling, six Groups of Notion, six Groups of Volition are to be explained following the calculation as mentioned earlier.

13. DISCERNMENT AND OTHER STATES

II. 13.1. That which is associated with Discernment, that which is not associated with Unbelief; that which is associated with Unbelief, that which is not associated with Discernment-these are to be explained following the calculation as mentioned earlier.

II.13.2. As Discernment paired with Unbelief is explained, in the same way Discernment paired with the remaining Impure states, Sensuous Attachement, Contact by knowledge, Contact by neither-knowledge-nor-non-knowledge, Absence of sense of shame, Absence of sense of fear are to be explained.

II. 13.3. That which is associated with Discerment, that which is not associated with Fury; that which is associated with Fury, that which is not associated with Discernment-these are to be explained following the calculation as mentioned earlier.

II. 13.4. As Discernment paired with Fury is explained, in the same way Discernment paired with the remaining Minor Impure states, Attachment for Immaterial existence, Doubt, five Views, Contact by knowledge, six Groups of Craving are to be explained.

II. 13.5. That which is associated with Discernment, that which is not associated with Attachment for Material existence; that which is associated with Attachment for Material existence, that which is not associated with Discernment-these are to be explained following the calculation as mentioned earlier.

II. 13.6. That which is associated with Discernment, that which is not associated with Contact by sensorial reaction; that which is associated with Contact by sensorial reaction, that which is not assoicated with Discernment-these are to be explained following the calculation as mentioned earlier.

II. 13.7. That which is associated with Discernment, that which is not associated with Verbal Contact; that which is associated with Verbal Contact, that which is not associated with Discernment-these are to be explained following the calculation as mentioned earlier.

II. 13.8. That which is associated with Discernment, that which is not associated with Faculty for pleasure; that which is associated with Faculty for pleasure, that which is not associated with Discernment-these are to be explained following the calculation as mentioned earlier.

II. 13.9. As Discernment paired with Faculty for pleasure is explained, in the same way Discernment paired with Faculty for indifference is to be explained.

II. 13.10. That which is associated with Discernment, that which is not associated with Faculty for pain; that which is associated with Faculty for pain, that which is not associated with Discernment-these are to be explained following the calculation as mentioned earlier.

II. 13.11. That which is associated with Discernment, that which is not associated with Faculty for satisfaction; that which is associated with Faculty for satisfaction, that which is not associated with Discernment-these are to be explained following the calculation as mentioned earlier.

II.13.12. As Discernment paired with Faculty for satisfaction is explained, in the same way Discernment paired with Faculty for dissatisfaction is to be explained.

II. 13.13. Discernment paired with Searching state of mind Investigation, Consciousness, six Groups of Contact, six Groups of Notion, six Groups of Volition are to be explained following the calculation mentioned earlier.

14. UNBELIEF AND OTHER STATES

II. 14.1. That which is associated with Unbelief, that which is not associated with Idleness; (under) 18 elements, 12 bases, and 5 aggregates, that which is associated with Unbelief etc. is to be explained in the same way as mentioned earlier.

That which is not associated with Idleness is included in what? In Idleness, Material existence, Unconditioned, and Mind-dissociated impressions, that is to say, 18 elements, 12 bases, and 5 aggregates.

II. 14. 2. That which is associated with Idleness, that which is not associated with Unbelief; (under) 18 elements, 12 bases, and 5 aggregates, that which is associated with Idleness is included in what? In Mind-state and Mental state, 8 elements, 2 bases and 4 aggregates. What is that which is left over? Idleness, Material existence, Unconditioned, and Mind-dissociated impressions; that is to say, 18 elements, 12 bases and 5 aggregates.

That which is not associated with Unbelief etc. is to be explained in the same way as mentioned earlier.

II. 14.3. As Unbelief paired with Idleness is explained, in the same way Unbelief paired with the remaining Impure states, Sensuous Attachment, Hatred, Contact by ignorance, Contact by neither-knowledge-nor-non-knowledge, Absence of sense of shame, Absence of sense of fear are to be explained.

II. 14.4. That which is associated with Unbelief, that which is not associated with Fury; that which is associated with Fury, that which is not associated with Unbelief-these are to be explained following the calculation as mentioned earlier.

II. 14.5. As Unbelief paired with Fury is explained, in the same way Unbelief paired with the remaining Impure states, Attachment for Immaterial existence, Doubt, five Views, Contact by knowledge, Six Groups of Craving are to be explained.

II. 14.6. That which is associated with Unbelief, that which is not associated with Attachment for Material existence; that which is associated with Attachment for Material existence, that which is not associated with

Unbelief-these are to be explained following the calculation as mentioned earlier.

II. 14.7. That which is associated with Unbelief, that which is not associated with Contact by sensorial reaction; that which is associated with Contact by sensorial reaction, that which is not associated with Unbelief-these are to be explained following the calculation as mentioned above.

II. 14.8. That which is associated with Unbelief, that which is not associated with Verbal Contact; that which is associated with Verbal Contact, that which is not associated with Unbelief-these are to be explained following the calculation as mentioned earlier.

II. 14.9. That which is associated with Unbelief, that which is not associated with Faculty for pleasure; that which is associated with Faculty for pleasure, that which is not associated with Unbelief-these are to be explained following the calculation as mentioned earlier.

II. 14.10. As Unbelief paired with Faculty for pleasure is explained, in the same way Unbelief paired with Faculty for indifference is to be explained.

II.14.11. That which is associated with Unbelief, that which is not associated with Faculty for pain; that which is associated with Faculty for pain, that which is not associated with Unbelief-these are to be explained following the calculation as mentioned earlier.

II. 14.12. That which is associated with Unbelief, that which is not associated with Faculty for satisfaction; that which is associated with Faculty for satisfaction, that which is not associated with Unbelief-these are to be explained following the calculation as mentioned earlier.

II. 14.13. As Unbelief paired with Faculty for satisfaction is explained, in the same way Unbelief paired with Searching state of mind Investigation, Consciousness, six

Groups of Consciousness, six Groups of Contact, six Groups of Feeling, six Groups of Notion, six Groups of Volition are to be explained.

15. EYE-CONSCIOUSNESS AND OTHER STATES

II. 15.1. That which is associated with Eye-consciousness, that which is not associated with Visual Contact; (under) 18 elements, 12 bases and 5 aggregates, that which is associated with Eye- consciousness is included in what ? In Mental State, 1 element, 1 base and 3 aggregates. What is that which is left over? Eye-consciousness, Material existence, Unconditioned, and Mind-dissociated impressions, that is to say, 18 elements, 12 bases, and 5 aggregates.

That which is not associated with Visual Contact is included in what? In Visual Contact, Material existence, Unconditioned, and Mind-dissociated impressions; that is to say, 18 elements, 12 bases, and 5 aggregates.

II. 15.2. That which is associated with Visual Contact, the which is not associated with Eye-consciousness; (under) 18 elements, 12 bases, and 5 aggregates, that which is associated with Visual Contact is included in what? In Mind-state and Mental state with 3 elements, 2 bases and 4 aggregates. What is that which is left over? Visual Contact, Material existence, Unconditioned, and Mind-dissociated impressions; that is to say, 17 elements, 12 bases, and 5 aggregates.

That which is not associated with Eye-consciousness is included in what? In Eye-consciousness, Material existence, Unconditioned, and Mind-dissociated impressions; that is to says 18 elements, 12 bases, and 5 aggregates.

II. 15.3. As Eye-consciousness paired with Visual Contact is explained, in the same way upto Eye-consciousness paired with six Groups of Volition are to be explained following the calculation mentioned earlier.

II. 15.4. That which is associated with Eye-consciousness, that which is not associated with Feeling born of visual contact; (under) 18 elements, 12 bases and 5 aggregates, that which is associated with Eye-consciousness is included in what? In Mental state, 1 element, 1 base and 3 aggregates. What is that which is left over? Eye-consciousness, Material Existence, Unconditioned, and Mind-dissociated impressions; that is to say, 17 elements, 12 bases, and 5 aggregates.

That which is not associated with Feeling born of visual contact is included in what? In Feeling born of visual contact, Material Existence, Unconditioned, and Mind-dissociated impressions; that is to say, 17 elements, 12 bases, and 5 aggregates.

II. 15.5. That which is associated with Feeling born of visual contact, that which is not associated with Eye-consciousness; (under) 18 elements, 12 bases, and 5 aggregates, that which is associated with Feeling born of visual contact is included in what? In Mind-state and Mental state, 3 elements, 3 bases and 3 aggregates. What is that which is left over? Feeling born of visual contact, Material existence, Unconditioned, and Mind-dissociated impressions; that is to say, 17 elements, 12 bases and 5 aggregates.

That which is not associated with Eye-consciousness is included in what ? In Eye-consciousness, Material existence, Unconditioned, and Mind-dissociated impressions; that is to say, 18 elements, 12 bases, and 5 aggregates.

II. 15.6. As Eye-consciousness paired with Feeling born of visual contact is explained, in the same way upto Eye-consciousness paired with Feeling born of mental contact and six Groups of Notion are to be explained following the calculation mentioned earlier.

II. 15.7. That which is associated with Eye-consciousness, that which is not associated with Craving born of visual contact; (under) 18 elements, 12 bases and 5 aggregates, that which is associated with Eye-consciousness is included in what? In Mental state, 1 element, 1 base, and 2 aggregates. What is that which is left over ? Eye-consciousness, Material existence, Unconditioned, and Mind-dissociated impressions; that is to say, 18 elements, 12 bases, and 5 aggregates.

That which is not associated with Craving born of visual contact is included in what? In Craving born of visual contact, Material existence, Unconditioned, and Mind-dissociated impressions; that is to say, 18 elements, 12 bases and 5 aggregates.

II. 15.8. That which is associated with Craving born of visual contact, that which is not associated with Eye-consciousness; (under) 18 elements, 12 bases, and 5 aggregates, that which is associated with Craving born of visual contact is included in what? In Visual Contact, Mind-state and Mental state, 3 elements, 2 bases, and 4 aggregates. What is that which is left over? Craving born of visual contact, Material existence, Unconditioned and Mind-dissociated impressions; that is to say, 17 elements, 12 bases and 5 aggregates.

That which is not associated with Eye-concsciousness is included in what ? In Eye-consciousness, Material existence, Unconditioned, and Mind-dissociated impressions; that is to say, 18 elements, 12 bases, and 5 aggregates.

II.15.9. As Eye-consciousness paired with Craving born of visual contact is explained, in the same way upto Eye-consciousness paired with Craving born of mental contact is to be explained following the calculation mentioned earlier.

16. GROUPS OF CONSCIOUSNESS, CONTACT, FEELING, NOTION, VOLITION AND OTHER STATES

II. 16.1. As the category of Eye-consciousness is explained, in the same way five categories upto Mind-consciousness are to be explained following the calculation mentioned earlier.

II. 16.2. As the six categories of the six Groups of Consciousness are explained, in the same way upto six categories of six Groups of Contact are to be explained following the calculation mentioned earlier.

II. 16.3. That which is associated with Feeling born of visual contact, that which is not associated with Notion born of visual contact; (under) 18 elements, 12 bases and 5 aggregates, that which is associated with Feeling born of visual contact is included in what? In Mind-state and Mental state, 3 elements, 2 bases, and 3 aggregates. What is that which is left over? Feeling born of visual contact, Material existence, Unconditioned, and Mind-dissociated impressions; that is to say, 17 elements, 12 bases, and 5 aggregates.

That which is associated with Notion born of visual contact is included in what? In Notion born of visual contact, Material existence, Unconditioned and Mind-dissociated impressions; that is to say, 17 elements, 12 bases and 5 aggregates.

II. 16.4. That which is associated with Notion born of visual contact, that which is not associated with Feeling born of visual contact; (under) 18 elements, 12 bases and 5 aggregates, that which is Notion born of visual contact is included in what ? In Mind-state and Mental state, 3 elements, 2 bases, and 3 aggregates. What is that which is left over? Notion born of visual contact, Material existence, Unconditioned, and Mind-dissociated impressions; that is to say, 17 elements, 12 bases, and 5 aggregates.

That which is not associated with Feeling born of visual contact is included in what? In Feeling born of visual contact, Material existence, Unconditioned, and Mind-dissociated impressions; that is to say, 17 elements, 12 bases, and 5 aggregates.

II. 16.5. As Feeling born of visual contact paired with Notion born of visual contact is explained, in the same way upto Feeling born of visual contact paired with Notion born of mental contact are to be explained.

II. 16.6. That which is associated with Feeling born of visual contact, that which is not associated with Volition born of visual contact; (under) 18 elements, 12 bases, and 5 aggregates, that which is associated with Feeling born of visual contact is included in what? In Mind-state and Mental state, 3 elements, 2 bases and 3 aggregates. What is that which is left over? Feeling born of visual contact, Material existence, Unconditioned and Mind-dissociated impressions; that is to say, 17 elements, 12 bases, and 5 aggregates.

That which is not associated with Volition born of visual contact is included in what? In Volition born of visual contact, Material existence, Unconditioned, and Mind-dissociated impressions; that is to say, 17 elements, 12 bases, and 5 aggregates.

II. 16.7. That which is associated with Volition born of visual contact, that which is not associated with Feeling born of visual contact; (under) 18 elements, 12 bases, and 5 aggregates, that which is associated with Volition born of visual contact is included in what ? In Mind-state and

Mental state, 3 elements, 2 bases, and 4 aggregates. What is that which is left over? Volition born of visual contact, Material existence, Unconditioned, and Mind-dissociated impressions; that is to say, 17 elements, 12 bases, and 5 aggregates.

That which is not assoicatd with Feeling born of visual contact is included in what? In Feeling born of visual contact, Material existence, Unconditioned, and Mind-dissociated impressions; that is to say, 17 elements, 12 bases, and 5 aggregates.

II. 16.8. As Feeling born of visual contact paired with Volition born of visual contact is explained, in the same way upto Feeling born of visual contact paired with Volition born of mental contact are to be explained.

II. 16.9. That which is associated with Feeling born of visual contact, that which is not associated with Craving born of visual contact; (under) 18 elements, 12 bases and 5 aggregates, that which is associated with Feeling born of visual contact is included in what ? In Mind-state and Mental state, 3 elements, 2 bases, and 3 aggregates. What is that which is left over ? Feeling born of visual contact, Material existence, Unconditioned and Mind-dissociated impressions; that is to say, 17 elements, 12 bases and 5 aggregates.

That which is not associated with Craving born of visual contact is included in what ? In Craving born of visual contact, Material existence, Unconditioned, and Mind-dissociated impressions; that is to say, 18 elements, 12 bases and 5 aggregates.

II. 16.10. That which is associated with Craving born of visual contact, that which is not associated with Feeling born of visual contact; (under) 18 elements, 12 bases and 5 aggregates, that which is associated with Craving born of visual contact is included in what ? In Mind-state and

Mental state, 3 elements, 2 bases and 4 aggregates. What is that which is left over? Craving born of visual contact, Material existence, Unconditioned, and Mind-dissociated impressions; that is to say, 18 elements, 12 bases, and 5 aggregates.

That which is not associated with Feeling born of visual contact is included in what? In Feeling born of visual contact, Material existence, Unconditioned, and Mind-dissociated impressions, 17 elements, 12 bases, and 5 aggregates.

II. 16.11. As Feeling born of visual contact paired with Craving born of visual contact is explained, in the same way upto Feeling born of visual contact paired with Craving born of mental contact are to explained.

II. 16.12. As the category of Feeling born of visual contact is explained, in the same way five categories upto Feeling born of mental contact are to be explained following the calculation mentioned earlier.

II. 16.13. As the six categories of six Groups of Feeling are explained, in the same way upto six categories of six Groups of Notion and six categories of six Groups of Volition are to be explained following the calculation mentioned earlier.

II. 16.14. Thus in brief it is said that there are 16 sections. But when calculated in details, it is said that there are 88 sections.

At the end of last *chüan* it is said; this text i.e. *Abhidharmadhātukāyapādaśāstra,* belongs to the *Sarvāstivāda* school.

NOTES

In Chapter II the terms Associated and not Associated are used from the first to the sixteenth section for strictly mental states. particularly to explore that nature and interrelation of different states.

The first section deals with the mental categories discussed in the first chapter to determine that they are associated with how many of the five *vedanendriya*. It also takes into consideration that they are dissociated from how many of the *vedanendriya*. In the second section the mental categories are examined to determine that (1) they are associated with many of the six Groups of Consciousness and (2) they are not associated with how many of the six Groups of Consciousness. In a similar manner, in the Third section, the association and dissociation of the mental categories and the two *dharmas*, i.e., *āhrīkya* and *anapatrāpya* are analyzed. The treatment of *sampayutta and vippayutta* is found in the sixth chapter of the *Dhātukathā* in Pāli, which deals with the states associated with and dissociated from the aggregates, bases and elements.

Another method of inquiry adopted in the *Dhātukathā* is that the mutual relations of the categories are examined in terms of inclusion *(saṅgahita,* Skt, *saṃgṛhīta)* and non-inclusion (*asaṅgahita*, Skt. *asaṃgṛhīta)* of a particular state with reference to aggregates, bases and elements (see first chapter of the *Dhātukathā)*. In chapter 11 of the same text a combined form of catechism is presented which "tries to understand the association and dissociation of those states, which together with state of inquiry, are included in the same aggregate, same base, and same element" *(Dhātukathā* Intro, II). Again, the catechism of chapter 13 of the same determines the association and dissociation of those states, which, together with the state of inquiry, are not included in the same aggregate, same base and same element (see *ibid.)*.

A combined application of the above methods is adopted in section 4-16 of the IInd chapter of the *ADPS*. It exhibits inclusion and non-inclusion of the "intended" states in pairs in terms of aggregates bases, and elements, which are associated with states of inquiry and dissociated from other states. In this manner, the mutual relation of the following states in pairs are examined:

Section 4 - Feeling paired with other state

Section 5 - Notion paired with other state

Section 6- Volition paired with other state

Section 7 - Contact paired with other state

Section 8 - Attention paired with other state

Section 9 - Desire paired with other state

Section 10 - Approbation paired with other state

Section 11- Memory paired with other state

Section 12 - Concentration paired with other state

Section 13 - Discernment paired with other state

Section 14 - Unbelief paired with other state

Section 15 - Eye-consciousness paired with other state

Section 16 - Groups of Consciousness paired with other state

Groups of Contact paired with other state

Groups of Feeling paired with other state

Groups of Notion paired with other state

Groups of Volition paired with other state

1. Associated *(samprayukta, hsiang-ying)* means the mental states which are united together being similar to each other (*samaṃ prayuktatvāt*, *AKB*, p. 209). Those states have five eqalities in common :-

1) Identity of support *(āśrayasamatā)*
2) Identity of object *(ālambanasamatā)*
3) Identity of aspect *(ākārasamatā)*
4) Identity of time *(kālasamatā)*
5) Identity of number of substances *(dravyasamatā)*

For details, see *AKB, ibid.*

2. The mental states which do not possess the above five characteristics are known as "dissociated" *(vipryaukta, pu-hsiang-ying).*

3. The Basic Mind-state *(mahābhūmi)* comprises of the ten mental states like Feeling etc., which exist in every moment of the mind. These states are distinct in nature, but coexist in one and the same moment (*AKB,* 187). The Five Faculties for Feeling *(vedanendriya)* are the conditions for the arousing of *vedanā.* As *vedanā* is experienced by the *vedanendriyas,* the two cannot be associated i.e., they cannot have the five common characteristics mentioned above. The nine other *mahābhūmikadharmas,* however, are not conditioned by the *vedanendriyas,* and are associated with all of them.

4. According to the *ADPS,* the Impure mind-state (*kleśamahābhūmi*) consists of ten *caittas* like Unbelief etc. (see 1.3) which exist in every moment of the mind along with the ten *caittas* of the Basic mind- state. Although they are of different natures, they coexist in the same moment. These states are associated with ignorance of truth or application to wrong thing due to ignorance. For details see *AK.* 2.33, *AKB.* The Faculties for Feeling are sources of the impurities of mental states (see *AK.* II. 9 with *AKB*). So the feeling states being dissimilar to the *caittas* of the Impure Mind-state, cannot be associated with the latter.

5. The Minor Impure states *(parīttakleśamahābhūmi)* consist of the ten *caittas* like Fury etc. (see p.) which are small (*parītta*) or ' non-serious' by nature. These states combined with the ten Basic Mind-states are known as the *parīttakleśamahābhūmikacitta.* Not all of the *caittas* of the *parīttakleśamahābhūmikas* are associated with all of the *vedanendriyas.* Thus *parīttaklesamahābhūmikas, i.e., krodha, upanāha, pradāśa, īrṣyā* and *vihimsā* are associated with two of the *vedanendriyas,* i.e., *daurmanasyendriya* and *upekṣendriya;* in the first case they have dejection for their mode *(dainyākāravartī)* and both belong to the sphere of the *manas* (Cf. V.7); in the second case, all the *parīttas* are associated with *upekṣā* because when the series of the *kleśas* is broken, there is indifference (cf. *AK.* V.56). Again, *mrakṣa, māyā,* and *śāṭhya* are associated with three of the

vedanendriyas, i.e., *saurmanasyendriya*, *dauramanasyendriya* and *upekṣendriya*, and are dissociated from four of the *vedanendriyas*, i.e., *sukhendriya*, *saurmanasyendriya*, *daurmanasyendriya*, and *upekṣendriya*, and is dissociated from *duḥkhendriya*. The state of *mātsarya* is associated with two of the Faculties, i.e., *saurmanasyendriya* and *upekṣendriya*, and is dissociated from *sukhendriya*, *duḥkhendriya* and *dauramanasyendriya*.

6. Cf. *AK*. V.55-56 with *Sphutārthā*.

7. *AK*. V, 57 and *Sphutārthā*.

8. Cf. *AK*. III. 31, IV. 49 and *Sphutārthā*.

9. According to *AK*. V. 58, also *AKB*, p. 851 - *āhrīkya* and *anapatrāpya* are associated with all of the five *vedanendriyas*, because those two are *akuśalamahābhūmikas*.

10. The five kinds of bodily consciousness are associated with *sukhendriya*, *duḥkhendriya* and *upekṣendriya* only, as the later are born of bodily contacts (*upekṣendriya* is born of both bodily and mental contacts).

11. The Groups of Contact, Notion and Volition are associated with *saurmanasyendriya* and *daurmanasyendriya* as the later two are born of mental contact.

SELECT BIBLIOGRAPHY

Original Sources

SANSKRIT AND PALI

Abhidharmakośa and *bhāṣya* of Acharya Vasubandhu, Part I and II (ed) Swami Dwarikadas Sastri, Varanasi, 1981.

Abhidharmāmṛta of Ghoṣaka, (Tr) from Chinese into Sanskrit, by Shanti Bhiksu Sastri, Santiniketan, 1958.

Abhidharmasamuccaya by Asanga, Pradhan, Santiniketan, 1950.

Aṅguttaranikāya, (ed) Morris and Hardy in 5 Vols., PTS. 1985-1900.

Dhātukathā and *Puggalapaññatti,* (ed.) Bhinkkhu J. Kasyap, Bihar, 1960.

Dīghanikāya, (ed.) T.W. Rhys Davids and J.E. Carpenter in 3 Vols., PTS, 1890-1911.

Jñānaprasthānaśāstra, (Tr.) from Chinese into Sanskrit by Shanti Bhiksu Sastri, Santiniketan, 1955.

Mahāvyutpatti, Bibliotheca Buddhica XIII, 1911.

Majjhimanikāya, (ed.) Trenchner and Chalmers in 3 Vols., PTS 1889-99, reprinted 1948-51.

Saṃyuttanikāya, (ed.) Feer in 5 Vols., PTS 1884-98, reprinted 1960.

CHINESE

A-p'i-ta-mo-chieh-shen-tsu-lun, (tr) Hsüan-tsang, A.D. 663, T. 1540.

A-p'i-ta-mo-chü-she-lun, (tr) Hsüan-tsang, A.D, 651-54, T. 1558.

Taisho shinshu daizōkyo, (ed) Takakusu Junjiro, 55 Vols, (Tokyo, 1914-22)

Ch'eng-wei-shih-lun by Hsüan-tsang, A.D. 659, T. 1586.

Secondary Sources

Banerjee, A.C. : *Sarvāstivāda literature*, Calcutta, 1957.

Book of Analysis (Vibhaṅga), The Second Book of the *Abhidhamma Piṭaka* (Translated from the Pāli of the Burmese Chaṭṭhasaṅgīti Edition) Published for the Pali Text Society, London by Luzac and Co., London, 1969.

Beal, Samuel : *Si-yu-ki-Buddhist Records of the Western World*, Reprint, Delhi, 1981.

Carpenter, J.E. and Rhys Davids, T.W. (eds): *Dīgha Nikāya*, 3 Vols., PTS, 1889-1910.

Chalmers, R. Trenckner, V. and Rhys Davids, C.A.F. (eds): *Majjhima Nikāya*, 4 Vols., PTS, 1889-1925.

Chaudhury, Sukomala : *Analytical Study of the Abhidharmakośa*, Calcutta, 2nd ed., 1983.

Dutt, N. : *The Spread of Buddhism and the Buddhist Schools*, First Indian Edition, 1980.

Guenther, Herbert V. : *Philosophy and Psychology in the Abhidharma*, Motilal Banarasidass, Delhi,1957.

Halder, Aruna : *Some Psychological Aspects of Early Buddhist Philosophy based on Abhidharmakośa of Vasubandhu*, The Asiatic Society, Calcutta, 1981.

Hardy, E. and Morris, R. (ed) : *Aṅguttara Nikāya*, 6 Vols., PTS, 1885-1910.

Feer, L. and Rhys Davids, C.A.F. (eds) : *Saṃyutta Nikāya*, 6 Vols., PTS, 1884-1904.

Ganguly, Swati, *Treatise in Thirty Verses on Mere-Consciousness*, Delhi, 1992.

Hare, E.M. and Woodward, P.L. (tr.) : *The Book of Gradual Sayings* (*Aṅguttara Nikāya*), 5 Vols., PTS, 1932-1936.

Karunaratna, Upali : "*Dhātukāya*" In *Encyclopedia of Buddhism*, Vol. IV, Fascicle 4, Ed. A.W.P. Guruge and W.G. Weeraratne, 1989.

Law, Bimala Charan : *A History of Pāli Literature*, Indological book House, Delhi, 1983.

Masuda, J. : "Origins and doctrines of Ealry Buddhist Schools" in *Asia Major,* 2:1-78.

Mathews, R.H. : *Chinese-English Dictionary,* Cambridge, 1975.

Monier-Williams, Sir Monier : *A Sanskrit- English Dictionary,* Motilal Banarasidass, Delhi,1986.

Narada Maha Thera : *A Manual of Abhidhamma* (ed.) Pali Text with English translation, Sri Lanka, 1980.

Narada U. : *Discourse on Elements,* PTS, 1977.

Nariman, J.K. *Literary History of Sanskrit Buddhism,* Reprint, Delhi, 1972.

Nyanatiloka : *Buddhist Dictionary : Manual of Buddhist Terms and Doctrines,* Frewin and Co., Colombo, 1972.

Poussin, Louis de La Vallee: *Abhidharma-Kośabhāṣyam* (English translation by Leo M. Pruden) Vols. I, II, III and IV, Asian Humanities Press, Berkeley, California, 1989-90

Takakusu, J. : "On the Abhidharma Literature of the *Sarvāstivādins*" in the *Journal of Pali Text Society,* 1905.

Tatia : N. "Sarvāstivāda" in the *Nava Nalanda Mahavihara Research Publication,* Vol. II. p. 77.

Thera Nyanaponika : *Abhidhamma Studies- Researches in Buddhist Psychology,* Buddhist Publication Society, Kandy, Sri Lanka, 1985.

Upadhyaya, Baladev : *Bauddha - Darśana- Mīmāṃsā* (in Hindi), Varanasi, 1978.

Warder, A.K. : *Indian Buddhism,* Motilal Banarsidass, Delhi, 1980.

Watanabe Fumimaro : *Philosophy and its Development in the Nikāyas and Abhidhamma,* Motilal Banarasidass, Delhi, 1983.

Watanabe, K. And Takakusu, J. (eds): *Taisho Shinshu Daizokyo,* 55 Vols, Tokyo, 1924-1929.

Watts, T. : *On Yuan-Chuwang's travel in India,* Second Indian Edition, Delhi, 1973.

Winternitz, M. : *History of Indian Literature,* Reprint, Delhi, 1983.

有十二心。欲界繫善心。不善心。有覆無記心。無覆無記心。色界繫善心。有覆無記心。無覆無記心。無色界繫善心。有覆無記心。無覆無記心。及學心無學心。若學心。捨成就得不成就。如是十二心。幾捨成就得不成就。幾捨不成就得成就。若無學心。捨成就得不成就。如是十二心。幾捨成就得不成就。幾捨不成就得成就

若學心。捨成就得不成就。二心定捨成就得不成就。一心定捨不成就得成就。餘非捨成就得不成就。亦非捨不成就得成就若無學心。捨成就得不成就。一心定捨成就得不成就。二心定捨不成就得成就。二心或捨成就得不成就。二心或捨不成就得成就。五❷心非捨成就得不成就。亦非捨不成就得成就

有十二心。謂欲界繫善心。不善心。有覆無記心。無覆無記心。色界繫善心。有覆無記心。無覆無記心。無色界繫善心有覆無記心。無覆無記心。及學心。無學心。若學心。捨不成就得成就。如是十二心。幾捨不成就得成就。幾捨成就得不成就。若無學心。捨不成就得成就。如是十二心。幾捨不成就得成就。幾捨成就得不成就

若學心。捨不成就得成就或有二心定。捨不成就得成就。一心定捨成就得不成就。二心或捨不成就得成就。二心或捨成就得不成就。或有得一。都無所捨。五心非捨不成就得成就。亦非捨成就得不成就。若無學心。捨不成就得成就。一心定捨不成就得成就。二心定捨成就得不成❸就

*說一切有部識身足論卷第十六

No. 1540

阿毘達磨界身足論卷上

尊者世友造

❸三藏法師玄奘奉　詔譯

本事品第一

三地各十種　五煩惱五見
五觸五根法　六六身相應

有十大地法。十大煩惱地法。十小煩惱地法。五煩惱。五見。五觸。五根。五法。六識身。六觸身。六受身。六想身。六思身。六愛身。十大地法云何。一受。二想。三思。四觸。五作意。六欲。七勝解。八念。九三摩地。十慧。十大煩惱地法云何。一不信。二懈怠三失念。四心亂。五無明。六不正知。七非理作意。八邪勝解。九掉舉。十放逸。十小煩惱地法云何。一忿。二恨。三覆。四惱。五嫉。六慳。七誑。八❹諂。九憍。十害。五煩惱云何。一欲貪。二色貪。三無色貪。四瞋。五疑。五見云何。一有身見。二邊執見。三邪見。四見取。五戒禁取。五觸云何。一有對觸。二增語觸。三明觸。四無明觸。五非明非無明觸。五根云何。一樂根。二苦根。三喜根。四憂根。五捨根。五法云何。一尋。二伺。三識。四無慚。五無愧。六識身云何。一眼識。二耳識。三鼻識。四舌識。五身識。六意識。六觸身云何。一眼觸。二耳觸。三鼻觸。四舌觸。五身觸。六意觸。六受身云何。一眼觸所生受。二耳觸所生受。三鼻觸所生受。四舌觸所生受。五身觸所生受。六意觸所生受。六想身云何。一眼觸所生想。二耳觸所生想。三鼻觸所生想。四舌觸所生想。五身觸所生想。六意觸所生想。六思身云何。一眼觸所生思。二耳觸所生思。三鼻觸所生思。四舌觸所生思。五身觸所生思。六意觸所生思。六愛身云何。一眼觸所生愛。二耳觸所生愛。三鼻觸所生愛。四舌觸所生愛。五身觸所生愛。六意觸所生愛。受云何。謂受等受各等受已受當受。受所攝是名受。想云何。謂想等想現想已想當想。是名想。思云何。謂思等思現思已思當思。思所攝造心意業。是名思。觸云何。謂觸等觸現觸已觸當觸是名觸。作意云何。謂心引於隨引等隨引。現作意已作意當作意。警覺心是名作意。欲云何。謂欲能欲性。現欲性。喜樂性。趣向性。希欲性。欣求性。欲有所作性是名欲。勝解云何。謂心勝解性。已勝解當勝解。是名勝解。念云何。謂念隨念別念憶念。憶念性不忘性。不忘法不失性。不失法不忘失性。心明記是名念。三摩地云何。謂心住等住。現住近住。不亂不散。攝持寂止等持。心一境性。是名三摩地。慧云何。謂於法簡擇。最極簡擇極簡擇。法了相近了相等了相。聰叡通達。審察決擇。覺明慧行。毘鉢舍那是名慧。不信云何。謂不信不信性。不現信性。不印不可。不已委信不當委信。不現委信。令心不淨是名不信。懈怠云何。謂不精進性。劣精進性。

*❶詔＝詔〇　*❷藏三＋(唐)❸　❹註夾(覺意)(成就)＋就〇　❺亙一(心)❻

味精進性。障礙精進。止息精進。心不勇悍。不已勇悍。不當勇悍。是名懈怠。失念云何。謂空念性。虛念性。忘念性。失念性。心不明記性。是名失念。心亂云何。謂心散性。心亂性。心異念性。心迷亂性。心不一境性。不住一境性。是名心亂。無明云何。謂三界無智。不正知云何。謂非理所引慧。非理作意云何。謂染污作意。邪勝解云何。謂染污作意相應。心勝解心印順。是名邪勝解。掉舉云何。謂心不寂靜。不極寂靜。不寂靜性。囂舉等囂舉。心囂舉性。是名掉舉。放逸云何。謂於斷不善法引集善法。不堅作。不恒常作。不親不近。不修不習。是名放逸。忿云何。謂忿等忿遍忿極忿。已忿當忿是名忿。恨云何。謂心結恨。等遍結恨。心怨結性是名恨。覆云何。謂隱所作罪。惱云何。謂心憤惱。堅執尤蛆。心佷戾性。是名惱。嫉云何。謂心不忍他之榮利。慳云何。謂於財法心著不捨。誑云何。謂矯惑他。諂云何。謂心曲。憍云何。謂如有一作如是念。我具妙色財位。技藝淨命功德。形貌端嚴衆所樂見。由此因緣便起憍傲極憍傲。醉悶等醉悶。矓眩等矓眩。心躭傲性是名憍。害云何。謂於有情樂爲捶撻諸損惱事是名害。欲貪云何。謂於諸欲起貪等貪。執藏防護愛樂耽著。是名欲貪。色貪云何。謂於諸色起貪等貪。執藏防護愛樂耽著。是名色貪。無色貪云何。謂於諸無色起貪等貪。執藏防護。愛樂耽著。是名無色貪。瞋云何。謂於有情欲爲逼害。內懷栽櫱極瞋恚遍瞋恚。等瞋恚。瞋極瞋意憤恚現瞋

恚已瞋恚當瞋恚。是名瞋。疑云何。謂於諸諦猶豫。有身見云何。謂於五取蘊等。隨觀執我或我所由此起。忍樂慧觀見。是名有身見。邊執見云何。謂於五取蘊等。隨觀執或斷或常。由此起忍樂慧觀見。是名邊執見。邪見云何。謂謗因謗果。或謗作用。或壞實事。由此起忍樂慧觀見。是名邪見。見取云何。謂於五取蘊等。隨觀執爲最爲勝爲妙第一。由此起忍樂慧觀見。是名見取。戒禁取云何。謂於五取蘊等。隨觀執爲清淨爲解脫爲出離。由此起忍樂慧觀見。是名戒禁取。有對觸云何。謂五識相應觸。增語觸云何。謂意識相應觸。明觸云何。謂無漏觸。無明觸云何。謂染污觸。非明非無明觸云何。謂不染有漏觸。樂根云何。謂觸順樂受。觸者所起身心樂平等受。受所攝是名樂根。苦根云何。謂觸順苦受。觸者所起身苦不平等受。受所攝是名苦根。喜根云何。謂觸順喜受。觸者所起心喜平等受。受所攝。是名喜根。憂根云何。謂觸順憂受。觸者所起心憂不平等受。受所攝。是名憂根。捨根云何。謂觸順不苦不樂受。觸者所起身心捨非平等非不平等受。受所攝。是名捨根。尋云何。謂心推覓遍推覓顯示極顯示。現前顯示。尋求遍尋求。算計遍算計。搆畫遍搆畫。分別等分別。等分別性是名尋。伺云何。謂心巡行遍巡行。隨遍巡行。伺察遍伺察。隨遍伺察。隨轉隨流。隨屬彼性是名伺。識云何。謂六識身。所謂眼識乃至意識。無慚云何。謂無慚無所慚無別慚。無羞無所羞無別羞。無敬無所敬無別敬。

無自在無所自在無別自在。無所畏憚自在而轉。是名無慚。無愧云何。謂無愧無所愧無別愧。無恥無所恥無別恥。於罪不怖性。於罪不畏性。於諸罪中不見怖畏。是名無愧。眼識云何。謂眼及色爲緣所生眼識。此中眼爲增上色爲所緣。於眼所識色所有了別。各別了別。是名眼識。耳鼻舌身意識云何。謂意及法爲緣所生意識。此中意爲增上法爲所緣。於意所識法所有了別。各別了別。是名意識。眼觸云何。謂眼及色爲緣生於眼識。三和合故觸。此中眼爲增上色爲所緣。於眼所識色諸觸等觸現觸已觸當觸。是名眼觸。耳鼻舌身意觸云何。謂意及法爲緣生於意識。三和合故觸。此中意爲增上法爲所緣。於意所識法諸觸等觸現觸已觸當觸。是名意觸。眼觸所生受云何。謂眼及色爲緣生於眼識。三和合故觸。觸爲緣受。此中眼爲增上色爲所緣。眼觸爲因。眼觸爲集。眼觸種類。眼觸爲緣。眼觸所生。作意相應。於眼所識色諸受等受各別等受已受當受受所攝。是名眼觸所生受。耳鼻舌身意觸所生受云何。謂意及法爲緣生於意識。三和合故觸。觸爲緣受。此中意爲增上法爲所緣。意觸爲因。意觸爲集。意觸種類。意觸爲緣。意觸所生作意相應。於意所識法。諸受等受各別等受已受當受受所攝。是名意觸所生受。眼觸所生想云何。謂眼及色爲緣生於眼識。三和合故觸。觸爲緣想。此中眼爲增上色爲所緣。眼觸爲因。眼觸爲集。眼觸種類。眼觸爲緣。眼觸所生作意相應。

①邪＝耶【宋】 ②佷＝很【宋】【元】，愼【元】，很【明】 ③技＝伎【宋】 ④矓＝朦【明】* ⑤蛆＝佷【明】 ⑥等＝識【元】 ⑦忍＝思【宋】 ⑧顯＝煩【宋】

於眼所識色諸想等想各別等想。現前等想已想當想。是名眼觸所生想。耳鼻舌身意觸所生想云何。謂意及法爲緣生於意識三和合故觸。觸爲緣想。此中意爲增上法爲所緣。意觸爲因。意觸爲集。意觸種類。意觸爲緣。意觸所生作意相應。於意所識法。諸想等想各別等想。現前等想已想當想。是名意觸所生想。眼觸所生思云何。謂眼及色爲緣生於眼識。三和合故觸。觸爲緣思。此中眼爲增上色爲所緣。眼觸爲因。眼觸爲集。眼觸種類。眼觸爲緣。眼觸所生作意相應。於眼所識色。❶諸思等思各別等思。現前等思已思當思。思所攝造心意業。是名眼觸所生思。耳鼻舌身意觸所生思云何。謂意及法爲緣生於意識。三和合故觸。觸爲緣思。此中意爲增上法爲所緣。意觸爲因。意觸爲集。意觸種類。意觸爲緣。意觸所生作意相應。於意所識法。諸思等思各別等思。現前等思已思當思。思所攝造心意業。是名意觸所生思。眼觸所生愛云何。謂眼及色爲緣生於眼識。三和合故觸。觸爲緣故受。受爲緣愛。此中眼爲增上色爲所緣。於眼所識色。諸貪等貪。執藏防護。愛樂耽著。是名眼觸所生愛。耳鼻舌身意觸所生愛云何。謂意及法爲緣生於意識。三和合故觸。觸爲緣受。受爲緣愛。此中意爲增上法爲所緣。於意所識法。諸貪等貪。執藏防護。愛樂耽著。是名意觸所生愛

分別品第二中初門

門有八十八　初異類三門
謂受幷識身　及無慚無愧
餘門八十五　謂受等次第
相應不相應　一行界處蘊

五受根。謂樂根苦❷根喜根憂根捨根。大地法受與五受根。幾相應幾不相應。乃至意觸所生愛與五受根。幾相應幾不相應。大地法受五受根無相應者。皆不相應。大地法想五受根。一切相應。無不相應者。如想思觸作意欲勝解念三摩地慧亦爾。不信五受根。五根相應。五根不相應。如不信。餘大煩惱地法亦爾。忿恨惱嫉害。二根相應。謂憂捨。五根不相應。覆誑※諂三根相應。除樂苦。五根不相應。憍四根相應除苦。五根不相應。慳二根相應。謂喜捨。五根不相應。欲貪色貪。三根相應除苦憂。五根不相應。無色貪一根相應。謂捨。五根不相應。瞋三根相應。除樂喜。五根不相應。疑四根相應。除苦。五根不相應。五見中邪見。四根相應。除苦。五根不相應。餘四見三根相應。除苦憂五根不相應。有對觸三根相應除喜憂。四根不相應。除苦。增語觸四根相應除。苦三根不相應除喜憂。明觸三根相應。除苦憂。五根不相應。無明觸及非明非無明觸。五根相應。五根不相應。樂根無相應者。皆不相應。如樂根。苦根喜根憂根捨根亦爾。尋伺五根相應。三根不相應。除苦憂。識五根相應無不相應者。無慚無愧五根相應。五根不相應。眼識三根相應。除喜憂。五根不相應。如眼識耳鼻舌身識亦爾意識四根相應。除苦三根不相應。除喜憂。如六識身。六觸身六想身六思身亦爾。眼觸所生受五受根無相應者。皆不相應。如眼觸所生受餘受身亦爾眼觸所生愛二根相應。謂樂捨。五根不相應。如眼觸所生愛。耳鼻舌身觸所生愛亦爾。意觸所生愛三根相應。除苦憂五根不相應

分別品第二中第二門

六識身。謂眼識耳識鼻識舌識身識意識。大地法受與六識身。幾相應幾不相應。乃至意觸所生愛與六識身。幾相應幾不相應。大地法受六識身。一切相應。無不相應者。如大地法受。餘大地法亦爾不信六識相應。六識不相應。如不信。餘大煩惱地法亦爾。忿一識相應。謂意。六識不相應。如忿餘小煩惱地法亦爾。欲貪六識相應。六識不相應。如欲貪瞋亦爾。色貪四識相應。除鼻舌。六識不相應。無色貪疑一識相應。謂意。六識不相應。五見一識相應。謂意。六識不相應。有對觸五識相應除意。一識不相應。謂意。增語觸一識相應。謂意。五識不相應。除意。明觸一識相應。謂意。六識不相應。無明觸及非明非無明觸。六識相應。六識不相應。樂根捨根六識相應。六識不相應。苦根五識相應。除意。六識不相應。喜根憂根一識相應。謂意。六識不相應。尋伺六識相應。一識不相應。謂意。識法六識身。無相應者。皆不相應。無慚無愧。六識相應。六識不相應。眼識六識身無相應者。皆不相應。如眼識耳鼻舌身意識亦爾。眼觸一識相應。謂眼。五識不相應。除眼。如眼觸耳鼻舌身意觸隨所應

❶諸＝識㊂〔〕　❷根＝樂㊂宮

亦爾。如六觸身。六受身六想身六思身亦爾。眼觸所生❶愛一識相應。謂眼。六識不相應。如眼觸所生*愛。耳鼻舌身意觸所生❷愛隨所應亦爾

分別品第二中第三門

二法。謂無慚無愧。大地法受。與此二法。幾相應幾不相應。乃至意觸所生*愛。與此二法。幾相應幾不相應。大地法受。諸不善者二法相應。無不相應者。餘受無相應者。皆不相應。如大地法受。餘大地法亦爾。不信諸不善者二法相應。無不相應者。餘不信無相應者。皆不相應。如不信餘大煩惱地法亦爾。忿恨覆惱嫉慳害。皆二法相應。無不相應者。誑*諂憍諸不善者二法相應。無不相應者。餘誑*諂憍無相應者。皆不相應。欲貪瞋恚。俱二法相應。無不相應者。色貪無色貪。無相應者。俱不相應。疑諸不善者。二法相應。無不相應者。餘疑無相應者。定不相應。五見中二見無相應者。俱不相應。三見諸不善者。皆二法相應。無不相應者。餘三見無相應者。皆不相應。有對增語無明觸。諸不善者皆二法相應。無不相應者。餘三觸無相應者。皆不相應。明觸非明非無明觸。無相應者。俱不相應。樂根諸不善者。二法相應。無不相應者。餘樂根無相應者。定不相應。如樂根苦喜憂捨根亦爾。尋伺識法諸不善者。皆二法相應。無不相應者。餘尋伺識法無相應者。皆不相應。無慚與無愧定相應。無不相應者。與無慚定不相應。無相應者。無愧與無慚定相應。無不相應者。與無愧定不相應。無相應者。眼識諸不善者。二法相應。無不相應者。餘眼識無相應者。皆不相應。如眼識耳鼻舌身意識亦爾。如六識身。六觸身六受身六想身六思身亦爾。眼耳身意觸所生愛。諸不善者。皆二法相應。無不相應者。餘眼耳身意觸所生愛。無相應者。皆不相應。鼻舌觸所生愛。俱二法相應。無不相應者❸❹

說一切有部界身足論卷上

阿毘達磨界身足論卷中

尊者世友造

三藏法師玄奘奉　詔譯

❺❻分別品第二中第四門

受相應。想不相應。十八界十二處五蘊受相應。何所攝。謂心心所法。八界❼二處三蘊❽此何爲餘。謂受自性。色無爲心不相應行。十一界。十一處三蘊。想不相應。何所攝。謂想自性。色無爲心不相應行。十一界。十一處三蘊。此何所問。謂除受相應及想不相應❽法。卽除一切法十八界十二處五蘊❾此下二事雖各除一而文影略顯各除二不爾不❾應除一切法受等自體不被除故。想相應。受不相應。十八界十二處五蘊想相應。何所攝。謂心心所法。八界二處三蘊。此何爲餘。謂想自性。色無爲心不相應行十一界十一處三蘊。受不相應。何所攝。謂受自性。色無爲。心不相應行。十一界十一處三蘊。此何所問。謂除想相應及受不相應法。卽除一切法十八界十二處五蘊。如以受對想。乃至以受對慧亦爾。受相應不信不相應。十八界十二處五蘊受相應何所攝。謂心心所法。八界二處三蘊。此何爲餘。謂受自性。色無爲。心不相應行。十一界。十一處三蘊。不信不相應。何所攝。謂不信自性。色無爲心不相應行十八界十二處五蘊。此何所問。謂除受相應及不信不相應法。卽除一切法十八界十二處五蘊。不信相應。受不相應。十八界十二處五蘊不信相應。何所攝。謂心心所法。八界二處四蘊。此何爲餘。謂不信自性。色無爲心不相應行、十八界十二處五蘊。受不相應。何所攝。謂受自性。色無爲心不相應行十一界十一處三蘊。此何所問。謂除不信相應及受不相應法。卽除一切法十八界十二處五蘊。如以受對不信。對❿餘大煩惱地法欲貪瞋無明觸非明非無明觸無慚無愧亦爾。受相應忿不相應。十八界十二處五蘊受相應。何所攝。謂心心所法。八界二處三蘊。此何爲餘。謂受自性。色無爲心不相應行十一界十一處三蘊。忿不相應。何所攝。謂忿自性。色無爲心不相應行。十八界十二處五蘊。此何所問。謂除受相應及忿不相應法。卽除一切法十八界十二處五蘊。忿相應受不相應。十八界十二處五蘊忿相應。何所攝。謂心心所法。三界二處四蘊。此何爲餘。謂忿自性。色無爲心不相應行。十八界十二處五蘊受不相應。何所攝。謂受自性。色無爲心不相應行。

❶愛＝受【明】【元】* ❷愛＝受【明】 ❸ ❹ ❺不分卷【明】 ❻二＝三【元】 ❼此＝比【明】 ❽法＝行【元】 ❾此下乃至除故三十二字宋元明宮四本作註 ❾應＝懸【元】 ❿餘＝除【明】【宮】

十一界十一處三蘊。此何所問。謂除忿相應及受不相應法。即除一切法十八界十二處五蘊。如以受對忿。對除小煩惱地法無色貪疑五見明觸六受身亦爾。受相應色貪不相應十八界十二處五蘊受相應。何所攝。謂心心所法。八界二處三蘊。此何爲除。謂受自性。色無爲心不相應行十一界十一處三蘊色貪不相應。何所攝。謂色貪自性。色無爲心不相應行　十八界十二處五蘊。此何所問。謂除受相應及色貪不相應法　即除一切法十八界十二處五蘊。色貪相應受不相應十八界十二處五蘊色貪相應。何所攝。謂心心所法。六界二處四蘊。此何爲除。謂色貪自性。色無爲心不相應行。十八界十二處五蘊　受不相應。何所攝。謂受自性。色無爲心不相應行十一界十一處三蘊。此何所問。謂除色貪相應及受不相應法。即除一切法十八界十二處五蘊。受相應有對觸不相應。十八界十二處五蘊。受相應。何所攝。謂心心所法。八界二處三蘊。此何爲除。謂受自性。色無爲心不相應行。十一界十一處三蘊。有對觸不相應。何所攝。謂有對觸自性。色無爲心不相應行。十三界十二處五蘊。此何所問。謂除受相應及有對觸不相應法　即除一切法十八界十二處五蘊有對觸相應受不相應。十八界十二處五蘊有對觸相應。何所攝。謂心心所法。七界二處四蘊。此何爲除。謂有對觸自性。色無爲心不相應行。十三界十二處五蘊受不相應。何所攝。謂受自性。色無爲心不

相應行。十一界十一處三蘊。此何所問。謂除有對觸相應及受不相應法。即除一切法十八界十二處五蘊。受相應增語觸不相應。十八界十二處五蘊受相應。何所攝。謂心心所法。八界二處三蘊。此何爲除。謂受自性。色無爲心不相應行十一界十一處三蘊。增語觸不相應。何所攝。謂增語觸自性。色無爲心不相應行。十七界十二處五蘊。此何所問。謂除受相應及增語觸不相應法　即除一切法十八界十二處五蘊。增語觸相應受不相應。十八界十二處五蘊增語觸相應。何所攝。謂心心所法。三界二處四蘊。此何爲除。謂增語觸自性。色無爲心不相應行。十七界十二處五蘊受不相應。何所攝。謂受自性。色無爲心不相應行。十一界十一處三蘊。此何所問。謂除增語觸相應及受不相應法。即除一切法十八界十二處五蘊。受相應尋不相應。十八界十二處五蘊。受相應。何所攝。謂心心所法。八界二處三蘊。此何爲除。謂受自性。色無爲心不相應行。十一界十一處三蘊。尋不相應。何所攝。謂尋自性。色無爲心不相應行。十三界十二處五蘊。此何所問。謂除受相應及尋不相應法。即除一切法十八界十二處五蘊。尋相應。受不相應。十八界十二處五蘊。尋相應。何所攝。謂心心所法。八界二處四蘊。此何爲除。謂尋自性。色無爲心不相應行。十三界十二處五蘊受不相應。何所攝。謂受自性。色無爲心不相應行。十一界十一處三蘊。此何所問。謂除尋相應及受不相應法。即除一切法

十八界十二處五蘊。如以受對尋。對伺亦爾。受相應識不相應十八界十二處五蘊。受相應何所攝。謂心心所法八界二處三蘊。此何爲除。謂受自性。色無爲心不相應行。十一界十一處三蘊。識不相應。何所攝。謂識自性。色無爲心不相應行　十八界十二處三蘊。此何所問。謂除受相應及識不相應法。即除一切法十八界十二處五蘊。識相應。受不相應。十八界十二處五蘊識相應。何所攝。謂心所法。一界一處三蘊。此何爲除。謂識自性。色無爲心不相應行。十八界十二處三蘊。受不相應。何所攝。謂受自性。色無爲心不相應行。十一界十一處三蘊。此何所問。謂除識相應及受不相應法。即除一切法十八界十二處五蘊。受相應眼識不相應。十八界十二處五蘊受相應。何所攝。謂心心所法。八界二處三蘊。此何爲除。謂受自性。色無爲心不相應行。十一界十一處三蘊。眼識不相應。何所攝。謂眼識自性。色無爲心不相應行。十八界十二處五蘊。此何所問。謂除受相應及眼識不相應法。即除一切法十八界十二處五蘊。眼識相應。受不相應。十八界十二處五蘊眼識相應。何所攝。謂心心所法。一界一處三蘊。此何爲除。謂眼識自性。色無爲心不相應行。十八界十二處五蘊。受不相應。何所攝。謂受自性色無爲心不相應行。十一界十一處三蘊。此何所問。謂除眼識相應及受不相應法。即除一切法十八界十二處五蘊。如以受對眼識。乃至對意識亦爾。受相應眼觸不相應。十八

界十二處五蘊受相應。何所攝。謂心心所法。八界二處三蘊。此何爲餘。謂受自性。色無爲心不相應行。十一界十一處三蘊。眼觸不相應。何所攝。謂眼觸自性。色無爲心不相應行。十七界十二處五蘊。此何所問。謂除受相應及眼觸不相應法。 卽除一切法十八界十二處五蘊。眼觸相應。受不相應。十八界十二處五蘊。眼觸相應。何所攝。謂心心所法。三界二處四蘊。此何爲餘。謂眼觸自性。色無爲心不相應行。十七界❶十處五蘊。受不相應。何所攝。謂受自性色無爲心不相應行。十一界十一處三蘊此何所問。 謂除眼觸相應及受不相應法。 卽除一切法十八界十二處五蘊。如以受對眼觸。乃至對意觸亦爾。如以受對六觸身。對六想身六思身。廣說亦爾❷。

❸分別品第二中第五門

❹想相應 思不相應十八界十二處五蘊想相應。何所攝。謂心心所法。八界二處三蘊。此何爲餘。❺謂想自性。色無爲心不相應行。十一界十一處三蘊思不相應。何所攝。謂思自性。色無爲心不相應行。十一界十一處二蘊。此何所問。謂除想相應及思不相應法。卽除一切法十八界十二處五蘊 思相應。想不相應。十八界十二處五蘊思相應。何所攝。謂心心所法八界二處四蘊。此何爲餘。謂思自性色無爲心不相應行。十一界十一處二蘊想不相應。何所攝。謂想自性。色無爲心不相應行。十一界十一處三蘊。此何所問。謂除思❻相應及想不相應法 卽除一切法十八界十二處五蘊。如以想對思。乃至對慧亦爾。想相應不信不相應。十八界十二處五蘊想相應何所攝。謂心心所法。八界二處三蘊。此何爲餘。謂想自性。色無爲心不相應行。十一界十一處三蘊。不信不相應。何所攝。謂不信自性。色無爲心不相應行。十八界十二處五蘊。此何所問。謂除想。相應及不信不相應法。 卽除一切法十八界十二處五蘊。不信相應想不相應。十八界十二處五蘊。不信相應。何所攝。謂心心所法。八界二處四蘊。此何爲餘。謂不信自性。色無爲心不相應行。十八界十二處五蘊。想不相應。何所攝。謂想自性。色無爲心不相應行。十一界十一處三蘊。此何所問。謂除不信相應及想不相應法。卽除一切法十八界十二處五蘊。如以想對不信。對餘大煩惱地法欲貪瞋無明觸非明非無明觸無慚無愧亦爾。想相應。忿不相應。十八界十二處五蘊想相應。何所攝。謂心心所法。八界二處三蘊。此何爲餘。謂想自性。色無爲心不相應行。十一界十一處三蘊。忿不相應何所攝。謂忿自性。色無爲心不相應行。十八界十二處五蘊。此何所問。謂除想相應及忿不相應法。 卽除一切法十八界十二處五蘊。忿相應。想不相應。十八界十二處五蘊。忿相應。何所攝。謂心心所法三界二處四蘊。此何爲餘。 謂忿自性。 色無爲心不相應行。十八界十二處五蘊。想不相應何所攝。謂想自性。色無爲心不相應行 十一界十一處三蘊。 此何所問。 謂除忿相應及想不相應法。卽除一切法十八界十二處五蘊。 如以想對忿對餘小煩惱地法無色貪疑五見明觸六❼愛身亦爾。想相應。色貪不相應。十八界十二處五蘊想相應。何所攝。謂心心所法。八界二處三蘊。此何爲餘。謂想自性。色無爲心不相應行。十一界十一處三蘊。色貪不相應。何所攝。謂色貪自性。色無爲心不相應行。十八界十二處五蘊。此何所問。謂除想相應及色貪不相應法。 卽除一切法十八界十二處五蘊。色貪相應。 想不相應。十八界十二處五蘊。色貪相應。何所攝。謂心心所法。六界二處四蘊。此何爲餘。謂色貪自性。色無爲心不相應行。十八界十二處五蘊。想不相應。何所攝。謂想自性。色無爲心不相應行。十一界十一處三蘊。此何所問。謂除色貪相應想不相應。 卽除一切法十八界十二處五蘊。想相應。有對觸不相應。十八界十二處五蘊想相應。何所攝。謂心心所法。八界二處三蘊。此何爲餘。 謂想自性。 色無爲心不相應行。十一界十一處❽三蘊。有對觸❾不相應。何所攝。謂有對自性。色無爲心不相應行。十三界十二處五蘊。此何所問。謂除想相應及有對觸不相應法。 卽除一切法十八界十二處五蘊。有對觸相應。想不相應。十八界十二處五蘊。有對觸相應。何所攝。謂心心所法。七界二處四蘊。此何爲餘。謂有對觸自性。色無爲心不相應行。十三界十二處五蘊。想不相應。何所攝。謂想自性。色無爲心不相應行。十一界十一處三蘊。此何所問。謂除有對觸

❶十＋十(二)【宋】 ❷ ❸阿毘達磨界身足論卷上終【明】 ❹ ❺卷下首【明】 ❻明註曰想相應思南藏作受相應想 ❼明註曰謂想自性南藏作謂受自性 ❽相＝想【明】 ❾受＝受【宋】 ❿三蘊＝二蘊【元】【宮】,明註曰二蘊南藏作三蘊 多有對觸不相應何所攝謂 ⓫〔不相應何所攝謂有對〕－【宋】

相應及想不相應法。卽除一切法十八界十二處五蘊。想相應。增語觸不相應。十八界十二處五蘊想相應。何所攝。謂心心所法。八界二處三蘊。此何爲除。謂想自性。色無爲心不相應行。十一界十一處三蘊。增語觸不相應。何所攝。謂增語觸自性。色無爲心不相應行。十七界十二處五蘊。此何所問。謂除想相應及增語觸不相應法。卽除一切法十八界十二處五蘊。增語觸相應。想不相應。十八界十二處五蘊增語觸相應。何所攝。謂心心所法。三界二處四蘊。此何爲除。謂增語觸自性。色無爲心不相應行。十七界十二處五蘊。想不相應何所攝。謂想自性。色無爲心不相應行。十一界十一處三蘊。此何所問。謂除增語觸相應及想不相應法。卽除一切法十八界十二處五蘊

❶想相應。樂根不相應。十八界十二處五蘊想相應。何所攝。謂心心所法。八界二處三蘊。此何爲除。謂想自性。色無爲心不相應行。十一界十一處❷三蘊。樂根不相應。何所攝。謂樂根自性。色無爲心不相應行。十八界十二處五蘊。此何所問。謂除想相應及樂根不相應法。卽除一切法十八界十二處五蘊。樂根相應。想不相應。十八界十❸二處五蘊。樂根相應。何所攝。謂心心所法。八界❹二處三蘊。此何爲除。謂樂根自性。色無爲心不相應行。十八界十二處五蘊。想不相應。何所攝。謂想自性。色無爲心不相應行。十一界十一處❺三蘊。此何所問。謂除樂根相應及想不相應法。卽除一切法十八界十二處五蘊。如以想對樂根。對捨根亦爾想相應。苦根不相應。十八界十二處五蘊想相應何所攝。謂心心所法八界二處三蘊。此何爲除。謂想自性。色無爲心。不相應行。十一界十一處三蘊。苦根不相應何所攝。謂苦根自性。色無爲心不相應行。十八界十二處五蘊。此何所問。謂除想相應及苦根不相應法。卽除一切法十八界十二處五蘊。苦根相應。想不相應。十八界十二處五蘊苦根相應。何所攝。謂心心所法。七界二處三蘊。此何爲除。謂苦根自性。色無爲心不相應行。十八界十二處五蘊。想不相應。何所攝。謂想自性。色無爲心不相應行。十一界十一處三蘊。此何所問。謂除苦根相應及想不相應法。卽除一切法十八界十二處五蘊。想相應。喜根不相應。十八界十二處五蘊想相應。何所攝。謂心心所法。八界二處三蘊。此何爲除。謂想自性。色無爲心不相應行。十一界十一處三蘊。喜根不相應。何所攝。謂喜根自性。色無爲。心不相應行。十八界十二處五蘊。此何所問。謂除想相應及喜根不相應法。卽除一切法十八界十二處五蘊。喜根相應。想不相應。十八界十二處五蘊。喜根相應。何所攝。謂心心所法。三界二處三蘊。此何爲除。謂喜根自性。色無爲。心不相應行。十八界十二處五蘊。想不相應。何所攝。謂想自性。色無爲心不相應行。十一界十一處三蘊。此何所問。謂除喜根相應及想不相應法。卽除一切法十八界十二處五蘊。如以想對喜根。對憂根亦爾。以思對尋伺識法六識身六觸身六思身。皆如受門中說。唯於受處應說其想。想相應。眼觸所生受不相應。十八界十二處五蘊想相應。何所攝。謂心心所法。八界二處三蘊。此何爲除。謂想自性。色無爲心不相應行。十一界十一處三蘊。眼觸所生受不相應何所攝。謂眼觸所生受自性。色無爲心不相應行。十七界十二處五蘊。此何所問。謂除想相應及眼觸所生受不相應法。卽除一切法十八界十二處五蘊。眼觸所生受相應。想不相應。十八界十二處五蘊。眼觸所生受相應。何所攝。謂心心所法。三界二處三蘊。此何爲除。謂眼觸所生受自性。色無爲心不相應行。十七界十二處五蘊。想不相應。何所攝。謂想自性。色無爲心不相應行。十一界十一處三蘊。此何所問。謂除眼觸所❻生受相應及想不相應法。卽除一切法十八界十二處五蘊。如以想對眼觸所生受。乃至對意觸所生受。隨其所應廣說亦爾

分別品第二中第六門

思相應。觸不相應。十八界十二處五蘊思相應。何所攝。謂心心所法。八界二處四蘊。此何爲除。謂思自性。色無爲心不相應行。十一界十一處二蘊。觸不相應。何所攝。謂觸自性。色無爲心不相應行。十一界十一處二蘊。此何所問。謂除思相應及觸不相應法。卽除一切法十八界十二處五蘊。觸相應。思不相應。十八界十二處五蘊觸相應。何所攝。謂心心

❶明註曰想相應樂根南藏作受相應亦　❷明註曰三蘊樂根南藏作三蘊亦　❸二＝三㊄宮　❹二＝三宮　❺三＝五宮　❻〔生〕－宮

所法。八界二處四蘊。此何爲餘。謂觸自性。色無爲。心不相應行。十一界十一處二蘊。思不相應。何所攝。謂思自性。色無爲。心不相應行。十一界十一處二蘊。此何所問。謂除觸相應及思不相應法。卽除一切法十八界十二處五蘊。如以思對觸。乃至對慧亦爾。思相應。不信不相應。十八界十二處五蘊思相應。何所攝。謂心心所法。八界二處四蘊。此何爲餘。謂思自性。色無爲。心不相應行。十一界十一處❶二蘊。不信不相應。何所攝。謂不信自性。色無爲。心不相應行。十八界十二處五蘊。此何所問。謂除思相應及不信不相應法。卽除一切法十八界十二處五蘊。不信相應。思不相應。十八界十二處五蘊。不信相應。何所攝。謂心心所❷法。八界二處四蘊。此何爲餘。謂不信自性。色無爲心不相應行。十八界十二處五蘊。思不相應。何所攝。謂思自性。色無爲心不相應行。十一界十一處二蘊。此何所問。謂除不信相應及思不相應法。卽除一切法十八界十二處五蘊。如以思對不信。對餘大煩惱地法欲貪瞋無明觸非明非無明觸無慚無愧亦爾。思相應。忿不相應。十八界十二處五蘊思相應。何所攝。謂心心所法。八界二處四蘊。此何爲餘。謂思自性。色無爲心不相應行。十一界十一處二蘊。忿不相應。何所攝。❸謂忿自性。色無爲心不相應行。十八界十二處五蘊。此何所問。謂除思相應及忿不相應法。卽除一切法十八界十二處五蘊。忿相應。思不相應。十八界十二處五蘊。忿相應。何所攝。謂心心所法。三界二處四蘊。此何爲餘。謂忿自性。色無爲。心不相應行。十八界十二處五蘊。思不相應。何所攝。謂思自性。色無爲心不相應行十一界十一處二蘊此何所問。謂除忿相應及思不相應法。卽除一切法十八界十二處五蘊。如以思對忿。對餘小煩惱地法無色貪疑五見明觸六❹愛身亦爾。思相應。色貪不相應。十八界十二處五蘊思相應。何所攝。謂心心所❺法。八界二處四蘊。此何爲餘。謂思自性。色無爲心不相應行。十一界。十一處。二蘊。色貪不相應。何所攝。謂色貪自性。色無爲心不相應行。十八界十二處五蘊。此何所問。謂除思相應及色貪不相應法。卽除一切法十八界十二處五蘊。色貪相應。思不相應。十八界十二處五蘊。色貪相應。何所攝。謂心心所法。六界二處四蘊。此何爲餘。謂色貪自性。色無爲心不相應行。十八界十二處五蘊。思不相應。何所攝。謂思自性。色無爲心不相應行。十一界十一處二蘊。此何所問。謂除色貪相應及思不相應法。卽除一切法十八界十二處五蘊。思相應。有對觸不相應。十八界十二處五蘊思相應。何所攝。謂心心所法。八界二處四蘊。此何爲餘。謂思自性。色無爲心不相應行。十一界十一處二蘊。有對觸不相應。何所攝。謂有對觸自性。色無爲心不相應行。十三界十二處五蘊。此何所問。謂除思相應及有對觸不相應法。卽除一切法十八界十二處五蘊。有對觸相應。思不相應。十八界十二處五蘊。有對觸相應。何所攝。謂心心所法。七界二處四蘊。此何爲餘。謂有對觸自性。色無爲心不相應行。十三界十二處五蘊。思不相應何所攝。謂思自性。色無爲心不相應行。十一界十一處二蘊。此何所問。謂除有對觸相應及思不相應法。卽除一切法十八界十二處五蘊。思相應。增語觸不相應。十八界十二處五蘊。思相應如前。乃至二蘊增語觸不相應如前。乃至五蘊如思相應增語觸不相應如是。增語觸相應。思不相應隨所應當廣說。思相應。樂根不相應。樂根相應。思不相應。隨所應當廣說。如以思對樂根。對捨根亦爾。思相應苦根不相應。苦根相應思不相應。隨所應當廣說。思相應。喜根不相應。喜根相應。思不相應。隨所應當廣說。如以思對喜根。對憂根亦爾。以思對尋伺識法六識身六觸身六受身六想身。隨所應當廣說❻

說一切有部界身足論卷中

阿毘達磨界身足論卷下

尊者世友造

三藏法師玄奘奉　詔譯

❼分別品第二中第七門

觸相應。作意不相應。十八界十二處五蘊。觸相應如前。乃至二蘊。作意不相應。何所攝。謂作意自性。色無爲。心不相應行。十＊一界十一處二蘊。此何所問。謂除觸相應及作意不

❶二＝一【宮】　❷法＝攝【宮】＊　❸〔謂〕－【宮】＊　❹愛＝受【宮】　❺＊　❻＊　❼不分卷【宮】

相應法。即除一切法十八界十二處五蘊。作意相應。觸不相應。十八界十二處五蘊。作意相應。何所攝。謂心心所法。八界❶二處四蘊。此何爲除。謂作意自性。色無爲心不相應行。十一界十一處二蘊。觸不相應等如前說。如以觸對作意。乃至對慧亦爾。觸相應。不信不相應。不信相應。觸不相應。隨所應當廣說。如以觸對不信。對餘大煩惱地法欲貪瞋無慚無愧亦爾。觸相應忿不相應。忿相應觸不相應。隨所應當廣說。如以觸對忿。對餘小煩惱地法無色貪疑五見六愛身亦爾。觸相應。色貪不相應。色貪相應。觸不相應。隨所應當廣說。觸相應。樂根不相應。樂根相應。觸不相應。隨所應當廣說。如以觸對樂根。對捨根亦爾。觸相應。苦根不相應。苦根相應。觸不相應。隨所應當廣說。觸相應。喜根不相應。喜根相應。觸不相應。隨所應當廣說。如以觸對喜根。對憂根亦爾。以觸對尋伺識法六識身六受身六想身六思身。隨所應當廣說

分別品第二中第八門

作意相應。欲不相應。十八界十二處五蘊。作意相應等如前說。欲不相應。何所攝。謂欲自性。色無爲。心不相應行。十一界十一處二蘊。此何所問。如前說。欲相應。作意不相應。十八界十二處五蘊欲相應。何所攝。謂心心所法。八界二處四蘊。此何爲除。謂欲自性。色無爲。心不相應行。十一界十一處二蘊。作意不相應等如前說。如以作意對欲。乃至對慧亦爾。作意相應。不信不相應。不信相應。作意不相應。隨所應當廣說。如以作意對不信。對餘大煩惱地法欲貪瞋無明。觸非明非無明觸無慚無愧亦爾。作意相應。忿不相應。忿相應。作意不相應。隨所應當廣說。如以作意對忿。對餘小煩惱地法無色貪疑五見明觸六愛身亦爾。作意相應。色貪不相應。色貪相應。作意不相應。隨所應當廣說。作意相應。有對觸不相應。有對觸相應。作意不相應。隨所應當廣說。作意相應。增語觸不相應。增語觸相應。作意不相應。隨所應當廣說。作意相應。樂根不相應。樂根相應。作意不相應。隨所應當廣說。如以作意對樂根。對捨根亦爾。作意相應。苦根不相應。苦根相應。作意不相應。隨所應當廣說。作意相應。喜根不相應。喜根相應。作意不相應。隨所應當廣說。如以作意對喜根。對憂根亦爾。以作意對尋伺識法六識身六觸身六受身六想身六思身。隨所應當廣說

分別品第二中第九門

欲相應。勝解不相應。十八界十二處五蘊。欲相應等如前說。勝❷解不相應。何所攝。謂勝解自性。色無爲心不相應行。十一界十一處二蘊。此何所問。謂除欲相應及勝解不相應法。即除一切法十八界十二處五蘊勝解相應欲不相應。十八界十二處五蘊勝解相應。何所攝。謂心心所法。八界二處四蘊。此何爲除。謂勝解自性。色無爲。心不相應行。十一界十一處二蘊。欲不相應等如前說。如以欲對勝解。對念三摩地慧亦爾。欲相應。不信不相應。不信相應。欲不相應。隨所應當廣說。如以欲對不信。對餘大煩惱地法欲貪瞋無明觸非明非無明觸無慚無愧亦爾。欲相應。忿不相應。忿相應。欲不相應。隨所應當廣說。如以欲對忿。對餘小煩惱地法無色貪疑五見明觸六愛身亦爾。欲相應。色貪不相應。色貪相應。欲不相應。隨所應當廣說。欲相應。有對觸不相應。有對觸相應。欲不相應。隨所應當廣說。欲相應。增語觸不相應。增語觸相應。欲不相應。隨所應當廣說。欲相應。樂根不相應。樂根相應。欲不相應。隨所應當廣說。如以欲對樂根。對捨根亦爾。欲相應。苦根不相應。苦根相應。欲不相應。隨所應當廣說。欲相應。喜根不相應。喜根相應。欲不相應。隨所應當廣說。如以欲對喜根。對憂根亦爾。以欲對尋伺識法六識身六觸身六受身六想身六思身。隨所應當廣說

分別品第二中第十門

勝解相應。念不相應。十八界十二處五蘊。勝解相應等如前說。念不相應。何所攝。謂念自性。色無爲。心不相應行。十一界十一處二蘊。此何所問。如前說。念相應。勝解不相應。十八界十二處五蘊念相應。何所攝。謂心心所法。八界二處四蘊。此何爲除。謂念自性。色無爲。心不相應行。十一界十一處二蘊。勝解不相應等如前說。如以勝解對念。對三摩地慧亦爾。勝解相應。不信不相應。不信相應。勝解不相應。隨所應當廣說。如以勝解對不信。對餘大煩惱地法欲貪瞋無明觸

❶二＝一【宮】　❷解＝觸【宮】

非明非無明觸無慚無愧亦爾。勝解相應。忿不相應。忿相應。勝解不相應。隨所應當廣說。如以勝解對忿。對餘小煩惱地法無色貪疑五見明觸六愛身亦爾。勝解相應。色貪不相應。色貪相應。勝解不相應。隨所應當廣說。勝解相應。有對觸不相應。有對觸相應。勝解不相應。隨所應當廣說。勝解相應。增語觸不相應。增語觸相應。勝解不相應。隨所應當廣說。勝解相應。樂根不相應。樂根相應。勝解不相應。隨所應當廣說。如以勝解對樂根。對捨根亦爾。勝解相應。苦根不相應。苦根相應。勝解不相應。隨所應當廣說。勝解相應。喜根不相應。喜根相應。勝解不相應。隨所應當廣說。如以勝解對喜根。對憂根亦爾。以勝解對尋伺識法六識身六觸身六受身六想身六思身。隨所應當廣說

分別品第二中第十一門

念相應。三摩地不相應。十八界十二處五蘊。念相應等如前說。三摩地不相應。何所攝。謂三摩地自性。色無爲。心不相應行。十一界十一處二蘊。此何所問。如前說。三摩地相應。念不相應。十八界十二處五蘊。三摩地❶相應。何所攝。謂心心所法。八界二處四蘊。此何爲餘。謂三摩地自性。色無爲。心不相應行。十一界十一處二蘊。念不相應等如前說。如以念對三摩地。對慧亦爾。念相應。不信不相應。不信相應。念不相應。隨所應當廣說。如以念對不信。對餘大煩惱地法。欲貪瞋無明觸非明非無明觸無慚無愧亦爾。念相應。忿不相應。忿相應。念不相應。隨所應當廣說。如以念對忿。對餘小煩惱地法無色貪疑五見明觸六愛身亦爾。念相應。色貪不相應。色貪相應。念不相應。隨所應當廣說。念相應。有對觸不相應。有對觸相應。念不相應。隨所應當廣說。念相應。增語觸不相應。增語觸相應。念不相應。隨所應當廣說。念相應。樂根不相應。樂根相應。念不相應。隨所應當廣說。如以念對樂根。對捨根亦爾。念相應。苦根不相應。苦根相應。念不相應。隨所應當廣說。念相應。喜根不相應。喜根相應。念不相應。隨所應當廣說。如以念對喜根。對憂根亦爾。以念對尋伺識法六識身六觸身六受身六想身六思身。隨所應當廣說

分別品第二中第十二門

三摩地相應。慧不相應。十八界十二處五蘊。三摩地相應等如前說。慧不相應。何所攝。謂慧自性。色無爲。心不相應行。十一界十一處二蘊。此何所問。如前說。慧相應。三摩地不相應。十八界十二處五蘊慧相應。何所攝。謂心心所法。八界二處四蘊。此何爲餘。謂慧自性。色無爲心不相應行。十一界十一處二蘊。三摩地不相應等如前說。三摩地相應。不信不相應。不信相應。三摩地不相應。隨所應當廣說。如以三摩地對不信。對餘大煩惱地法欲貪瞋無明觸非明非無明觸無慚無愧亦爾。三摩地相應。忿不相應。忿相應。三摩地不相應。隨所應當廣說。如以三摩地對忿。對餘小煩惱地法無色貪疑五見明觸六愛身亦爾。三摩地相應。色貪不相應。色貪相應。三摩地不相應。隨所應當廣說。三摩地相應。有對觸不相應。有對觸相應。三摩地不相應。隨所應當廣說。三摩地相應。增語觸不相應。增語觸相應。三摩地不相應。隨所應當廣說。三摩地相應。樂根不相應。樂根相應。三摩地不相應。隨所應當廣說。如以三摩地對樂根。對捨根亦爾。三摩地相應。苦根不相應。苦根相應。三摩地不相應。隨所應當廣說。三摩地相應。喜根不相應。喜根相應。三摩地不相應。隨所應當廣說。如以三摩地對喜根。對憂根亦爾。以三摩地。對尋伺識法六識身六觸身六受身六想身六思身。隨所應當廣說

分別品第二中第十三門

慧相應。不信不相應。不信相應。慧不相應。隨所應❷當廣說。如以慧對不信。對餘大煩惱地法欲貪瞋無明觸非明非無明觸無慚無愧亦爾。慧相應。忿不相應。忿相應。慧不相應。隨所應當廣說。如以慧對忿。❸餘小煩惱地法無色貪疑五見明觸六愛身亦爾。慧相應。色貪不相應。色貪相應。慧不相應。隨所應當廣說。慧相應。有對觸不相應。有對觸相應。慧不相應。隨所應當廣說。慧相應。增語觸不相應。增語觸相應。慧不相應。隨所應當廣說。慧相應。樂根不相應。樂根相應。慧不相應。隨所應當廣說。如以慧對樂根。對捨根亦爾。慧相應。苦根不相應。苦根相應。慧不相應。隨所應當廣說。慧相應。喜根不相應。喜根相應。慧

❶相應＝應相㊂　❷當＝廣㊂　❸(對)＋餘㊂㊂

不相應。隨所應當廣說。如以慧對喜根、對憂根亦爾。以慧對尋伺識法六識身六觸身六受身六想身六思身。隨所應當廣說

分別品第二中第十四門

不信相應懈怠不相應。十八界十二處五蘊。不信相應等如前說。懈怠不相應。何所攝。謂懈怠自性。色無爲。心不相應行。十八界十二處五蘊。此何所問。如前說。懈怠相應。不信不相應。十八界十二處五蘊。懈怠相應。何所攝。謂心心所法八界二處四蘊。此何爲餘。謂懈怠自性色無爲心不相應行。十八界十二處五蘊。不信不相應等如前說。如以不信對懈怠。對餘大煩惱地法欲貪瞋無明觸。非明非無明觸無慚無愧亦爾。不信相應。怠不相應。怠相應。不信不相應。隨所應當廣說。如以不信對怠。對餘小煩惱地法無色貪疑五見明觸六愛身亦爾。不信相應。色貪不相應。色貪相應不信不相應。隨所應當廣說。不信相應。有對觸不相應。有對觸相應。不信不相應。隨所應當廣說。不信相應增語觸不相應。增語觸相應。不信不相應。隨所應當廣說。不信相應。樂根不相應。樂根相應。不信不相應。隨所應當廣說。如以不信對樂根。對捨根亦爾。不信相應。苦根不相應。苦根相應。不信不相應。隨所應當廣說。不信相應。喜根不相應。喜根相應。不信不相應。隨所應當廣說。如以不信對喜根。對憂根亦爾。以不信對尋伺識法六識身六觸身六受身六想身六思身。隨所應當廣說

分別品第二中第十五門

由斯理趣。共懈怠等諸差別門。應依前說一行方便。如理當思此諸門中。有差別者。相似異位。皆不應說。乃至眼識相應。眼觸不相應。十八界十二處五蘊。眼識相應。何所攝。謂心所法。一界一處三蘊。此何爲餘。謂眼識自性。色無爲。心不相應行。十八界十二處五蘊。眼觸不相應。何所攝。謂眼觸自性。色無爲。心不相應行。十七界十二處五蘊。此何所問。謂除眼識相應及眼觸不相應法。即除一切法十八界十二處五蘊。眼觸相應。眼識不相應。十八界十二處五蘊。眼觸相應。何所攝。謂心心所法。三界二處四蘊。此何爲餘。謂眼觸自性色無爲。心不相應行。十七界十二處五蘊。眼識不相應。何所攝。謂眼識自性。色無爲。心不相應行。十八界十二處五蘊。此何所問。謂除眼觸相應及眼識不相應法。即除一切法十八界十二處五蘊。如以眼識對眼觸。乃至對意觸六思身。隨所應當廣說。眼識相應。眼觸所生受不相應。十八界十二處五蘊眼識相應。何所攝。謂心所法。一界一處三蘊。此何爲餘。謂眼識自性。色無爲。心不相應行。十八界十二處五蘊。眼觸所生受不相應。何所攝。謂眼觸所生受自性。色無爲心不相應行。十七界十二處五蘊。此何所問謂除眼識相應及眼觸所生受不相應法。即除一切法十八界十二處五蘊。眼觸所生受相應。眼識不相應。十八界十二處五蘊。眼觸所生受相應。何所攝。謂心心所法。三界二處三蘊。此何爲餘。謂眼觸所生受自性。色無爲心不相應行。十七界十二處五蘊。眼識不相應。何所攝。謂眼識自性。色無爲心不相應行。十八界十二處五蘊。此何所問。謂除眼觸所生受相應及眼識不相應法。即除一切法十八界十二處五蘊。如以眼識對眼觸所生受乃至對意觸所生受六想身。隨所應當廣說。眼識相應。眼觸所生受不相應。十八界十二處五蘊。眼識相應。何所攝。謂心所法。一界一處三蘊。此何爲餘。謂眼識自性。色無爲。心不相應行。十八界十二處五蘊。眼觸所生*愛不相應。何所攝。謂眼觸所生*愛自性。色無爲。心不相應行。十八界十二處五蘊。此何所問。謂除眼識相應及眼觸所生*愛不相應法。即除一切法十八界十二處五蘊。眼觸所生*愛相應。眼識不相應。十八界十二處五蘊。眼觸所生*愛相應。何所攝。謂心心所法。三界二處四蘊。此何爲餘。謂眼觸所生*愛自性。色無爲。心不相應行。十八界十二處五蘊。眼識不相應。何所攝。謂眼識自性。色無爲心不相應行。十八界十二處五蘊。此何所問。謂除眼觸所生*愛相應及眼識不相應法。即除一切法十八界十二處五蘊。如以眼識對眼觸所生*愛乃至對意觸所生*愛亦爾

分別品第二中第十六門

如眼識門。如是乃至意識五門。隨所應當廣說。如六識身六門六觸身六門。隨所應當廣說。眼觸所生受相應。眼識所生想不相應。

十八界十二處五蘊。眼觸所生受相應。何所攝。謂心心所法。三界二處三蘊。此何爲餘。謂眼觸所生受自性。色無爲。心不相應行。十七界十二處五蘊。眼觸所生想不相應。何所攝。謂眼觸所生想自性。色無爲。心不相應行。十七界十二處五蘊。此何所問。謂除眼觸所生受相應。及眼觸所生想不相應法。卽除一切法十八界十二處五蘊。眼觸所生想相應。眼觸所生受不相應。十八界十二處五蘊。眼觸所生想相應。何所攝。謂心心所法。三界二處三蘊。此何爲餘。謂眼觸所生想自性。色無爲心不相應行。十七界十二處五蘊。眼觸所生受不相應。何所攝。謂眼觸所生受自性。色無爲心不相應行。十七界十二處五蘊。此何所問。謂除眼觸所生想相應及眼觸所生受不相應法。卽除一切法十八界十二處五蘊。如以眼觸所生受對眼觸所生想。乃至對意觸所生想亦爾。眼觸所生受相應。眼觸所生思不相應。十八界十二處五蘊。眼觸所生受相應。何所攝。謂心心所法。三界二處三蘊。此何爲餘。謂眼觸所生受自性。色無爲心不相應行。十七界十二處五蘊。眼觸所生思不相應。何所攝。謂眼觸所生思自性。色無爲心不相應行。十七界十二處五蘊。此何所問。謂除眼觸所生受相應及眼觸所生思不相應法。卽除一切法十八界十二處五蘊。眼觸所生思相應。眼觸所生受不相應。十八界十二處五蘊。眼觸所生思相應。何所攝。謂心心所法。三界二處四蘊。此何爲餘。謂眼觸所生思自性。色無爲心不相應行。十七界十二處五蘊。眼觸所生受不相應。何所攝。謂眼觸所生受自性。色無爲。心不相應行。十七界十二處五蘊。此何所問。謂除眼觸所生思相應及眼觸所生受不相應法。卽除一切法十八界十二處五蘊。如以眼觸所生受對眼觸所生思。乃至對意觸所生思亦爾。眼觸所生受相應。眼觸所生*愛不相應。十八界十二處五蘊。眼觸所生受相應。何所攝。謂心心所法。三界二處三蘊。此何爲餘。謂眼觸所生受自性。色無爲心不相應行。十七界十二處五蘊。眼觸所生受不相應。何所攝。謂眼觸所生*愛自性。色無爲。心不相應行。十八界十二處五蘊。此何所問。謂除眼觸所生*愛相應及眼觸所生*愛不相應法。卽除一切法十八界十二處五蘊。眼觸所生*愛相應。眼觸所生受不相應。十八界十二處五蘊。眼觸所生*愛相應。何所攝。謂心心所法。三界二處四蘊。此何爲餘。謂眼觸所生*愛自性。色無爲心不相應行。十八界十二處五蘊。眼觸所生受不相應。何所攝。謂眼觸所生受自性。色無爲。心不相應行。十七界十二處五蘊。此何所問。謂除眼觸所生*愛相應。及眼觸所生受不相應法。卽除一切法十八界十二處五蘊。如以眼觸所生受對眼觸所生*愛。乃至對意觸所生*愛亦爾。如眼觸所生受門。如是乃至意觸所生受五門。隨所應當廣說。如六受身六門。六想身六門六思身六門。隨所應當廣說。如是略說有十六門。若廣說有八十八門

說一切有部界身足論卷下

界身足論後序

沙門釋基製

界身足論者。說一切有部發智六足之一足也。詳夫邃旨沖微。非大理無以揚其奧。梵言幽祕。非上哲何以釋其眞。是以夕霏金容。晨馳白馬。譯經者結轍。津義者聯蹤。至於婆沙八蘊。缺五蘊之幽趣。發智六足。無五足之玄文。餘旨雖存。尚多紕綎。故使三秦匠彥穿鑿於異端。九土緇英滯惑於眞僞。故我親教三藏法師玄奘。業該群籍。志隆弘撫。欲使有宗俊穎。不延頸於五天。對法雄傑。恢慷慨於四主。遂以大唐龍朔三年六月四日。於玉華宮八桂亭。終譯此論。原其大本。頌有六千。後以文繁。或致刪略爲九百頌五百頌者。今此所翻有八百三十頌。文遺廣略義雖增減。詳其論始。說能仁。大德流通遂師名稱。尊者世友之所作也。旣而道滿待機。因四佇列神功妙思。緊可殫言。但甚慮遊操觚。謬倍函丈。承暉彫斷受旨執文。惟恐愛海波騰。玄源祕洩。嗚法舟之淪喪。故敍其時事云

❶不＝所㊂㊄ ❷問＝問㊄ ❸說一切有部＝阿毘達磨㊂ [illegible]

ABHIDHARMA-DHĀTUKĀYA-PĀDAŚĀSTRA
Sanskrit-Chinese-English Vocabulary

I *bhūmi ti* 地

Mind-state

tisra bhumayaḥ

san-ti 三地

Three Mind-states

mahābhūmikādharmas ta-ti-fa 大地法

Basic states

kleśamahābhūmikadharmas ta-fan-nao-ti-fa

Impure states 大煩惱地法

parīttakleśamahābhūmikadharmas hsiao-fan-nao-ti-fa

Minor Impure states 小煩惱地法

II *daśa mahābhūmikadharmāḥ*

shih-ta-ti-fa 十大地法

Ten Basic states

vedanā shou 受

Feeling

saṃjñā hsiang 想

Notion

cetanā szu 思

Volition

sparśa ch'u 觸

Contact

manaskāra tsuo-yi 作意

Attention

chanda yü 欲

Desire

adhimokṣa sheng-chiai 勝解

Approbation

smṛti nien 念

Memory

samādhi san-mo-ti 三摩地

Concentration

mati, prajñā hui 慧

Discernment

III *daśa kleśamahābhūmikadharmāḥ*

shih-ta-fan-nao-ti-fa 十大煩惱地法

Ten Impure states

āśraddhya pu-hsin 不信

Unbelief

kauśīdya hsia-tai 懈怠

Idleness

muṣitāsmṛti shih-nien 失念

Forgetfulness

vikṣepa hsin-luan 心亂

Distraction

avidyā wu-ming 無明

Ignorance

asaṃprajanya pu-cheng-chih 不正知

Non-discernment

ayoniśomanaskāra fei-li-tso-i 非理作意

Wrong Attention

mithyādhimokṣa hsieh-sheng-chieh 邪勝解

False Resolve

auddhatya tiao-chü 掉舉

Restlessness

pramāda fang-i 放逸

Carelessness

IV *daśa parīttakleśamahābhūmikāḥ*

shih-hsiao-fan-nao-ti-fa 十小煩惱地法

Ten Minor Impure states

krodha fen 忿

Fury

upanāha hen 恨

Enmity

mrakṣa fu 覆

Hypocricy

pradāśa nao 惱

Vexation

irṣyā chi, tsi 嫉

Envy

mātsarya chien 慳

Parsimony

śāṭhya k'uang 誑

Deception

māyā ch'an 諂
Duplicity

mada chueh 憍
Pride

vihiṃsā hai 害
Harmfulness

V *kleśa fan-nao* 煩惱
Moral impurities

pañca kleśāḥ

wu-fan-nao 五煩惱
Five Moral impurities

kāmarāga yu-t'an 欲貪
Sensuous Attachment

rūparāga se-t'an 色貪
Attachment for material exixtense

arūparāga wu-se-t'an 無色貪
Attachment for immaterial existence

dveṣa ch'en 瞋
Hatred

vicikitsā i 疑

Doubt

VI *dṛṣṭi chien* 見

View

pañca dṛṣtayaḥ

wu-chien 五見

Five Views

satkāyadṛṣṭi yu-sheng-chien 有身見

Personality belief

antagrāhadṛṣṭi pien-chih 邊執

Viewpoint of nihilism or eternalism

mithyādṛṣṭi hsieh-chien 邪見

Wrong View

dṛṣṭiparāmarśa chien-chu 見取

Wrong View as in attachment to a particular view

śīlavrataparāmarśa chiai-chin-chu 戒禁取

Wrong view as in attachment to mere rules and rituals

VII *sparśa ch'u* 觸

Contact

pañca sparśāḥ

wu-ch'u 五觸

Five Contacts

pratighasparśa yu-tui-ch'u 有對觸

Contact by sensorial reaction

adhivacanasparśa tsing-yu-ch'u 增語觸

Verbal Contact

vidyāsparśa ming-ch'u 明觸

Contact by knowledge

avidyāsparśa wu-ming-ch'u 無明觸

Contact by ignorance

na-vidyā-nāvidyā-sparśa fei-ming-fei-wu-ming-ch'u
非明非無明觸

Contact by neither-knowledge-nor-non-knodwledge

VIII *indriya ken* 根

Faculty

pañca indriyāṇi

wu-ken 五根

Five Faculties

sukhendriya le-ken 樂根

Faculty for feeling pleasure

duḥkhendriya k'u-ken 苦根

Faculty for feeling pleasure

saurmanasyendriya hsi-ken 喜根

Faculty for feeling satisfaction

daurmanasyendriya yu-ken 憂根

Faculty for feeling dissatisfaction

upekṣendriya she-ken 捨根

Faculty for feeling indifference

IX *pañcadharmāḥ wu-fa* 五法

Five dharmas

vitarka hsin 尋

Intellectual reflection

vicāra tz'u 伺

Investigation

vijñāna shih 識

Consciousness

āhrīkya wu-ts'an 無慚

Absence of sense of shame

anapatrāpya wu-k'uei 無愧

Absence of fear of blame

X *vijñānakāya shih-shen* 識身

Groups of knowledge

ṣaṭ vijñānakāyāḥ liu-shih-shen 六識身

Six Groups of knowledge

cakṣurvijñāna yen-shih 眼識

Eye-consciousness

śrotravijñāna erh-shih 耳識

Ear-consciousness

ghrāṇavijñāna p'i-shih 鼻識

Olfactory consciousness

jihvāvijñāna she-shih 舌識

Gustatory consciousness

kāyavijñāna shen-shih 身識

Body-consciousness

manovijñāna i-shih 意識

Mind-consciousness

XI. *sparśakāya ch'u-shen* 觸身

Group of contact

ṣaṭ sparsakāyāḥ

liu-ch'u-shen 六觸身

Six Groups of Contact

cakṣusparśa yen-ch'u 眼觸

Visual Contact

śrotrasparśa erh-ch'u 耳觸

Contact by hearing

ghrāṇasparśa p'i-ch'u 鼻觸

Contact by smelling

jihvāsparśa she-ch'u 舌觸

Contact by tasting

kāyasparśa shen-ch'u 身觸

Tactile Contact

manaḥśparsa i-ch'u 意觸

Mental Contact

XII *vedanākāya shou-shen* 受身

Group of Feeling

ṣaṭ vedanākāyāḥ

liu-shou-shen 六受身

Six Groups of Feeling

cakṣusparśajā vedanā yen-ch'u-suo-sheng-shou

眼觸所生受

Feeling born of contact with the organ of view along with its object

śrotrasparśajā vedanā erh-ch'u-suo-sheng-shou

耳觸所生受

Feeling born of contact with the organ of hearning along with its object.

ghrāṇasparśajā vedanā p'i-ch'u-suo-sheng-shou

鼻觸所生受

Feeling born of contact with the organ of smelling along with its object.

Jihvāsparśajā vedanā she-ch'u-suo sheng-shou

舌觸所生受

Feeling born of contact with the organ of tasting along with its object.

kāyasparśajā vedanā shen-ch'u-suo-sheng-shou

身觸所生受

Feeling born of contact with the body along with its object.

manaḥsparśajā vedanā i-ch'u-suo-sheng-shou

意觸所生受

Feeling born of contact with the mind along with its object.

XIII *saṃjñākāya hsiang-shen* 想身

Group of Notion

ṣaṭ saṃjñākāyāḥ

liu-hsiang-shen 六想身

Six Groups of Notion

cakṣuparśaja saṃjñā yen-ch'u-suo-sheng-hsiang

眼觸所生想

Notion born of contact with eye

śrotrasparśajā saṃjñā erh-ch'u-sheng-hsiang

耳觸所生想

Notion born of contact with ear

ghrāṇasparśajā saṃjñā p'i-ch'u-suo-sheng-hsiang

鼻觸所生想

Notion born of contact with nose

jihvāsparśajā saṃjñā she-ch'u-suo-sheng-hsiang

舌觸所生想

Notion born of contact with tongue

kāyasparśajā saṃjñā shen-ch'u-suo-sheng-hsiang

身觸所生想

Notion born of contact with body

manaḥsparśajā saṃjñā i-ch'u-suo-sheng-hsiang

意觸所生想

Notion born of contact with mind

XIV *cetanākāya szu-shen* 思身

Group of Volition

ṣaṭ cetanākāyāḥ

liu-szu-shen 六思身

Six Groups of Volition

cakṣusparśajā cetanā yen-ch'u-suo-sheng-szu

眼觸所生思

Volition born of visual contact

śrotrasparśajā cetanā erh-ch'u-suo-sheng-szu

耳觸所生思

Volition born of contact with ear

ghrāṇasparśajā cetanā p'i-ch'u-suo-sheng-szu

鼻觸所生思

Volition born of contact with nose

jihvāsparśajā cetana she-ch'u-suo-sheng-szu

舌觸所生思

Volition born of contact with body

kāyasparśajā cetanā shen-ch'u-suo-sheng-szu

身觸所生思

Volition born of contact with body

manaḥsparśajā cetanā i-ch'u-suo-sheng-szu

意觸所生思

Volition born of contact with mind

XV *tṛṣṇākaya ai-shen* 愛身

Group of Craving

ṣaṭ tṛṣṇākāyāḥ

liu-ai-shen 六愛身

Six Groups of Craving

cakṣusparśajā tṛṣṇā yen-ch'u-suo-sheng-ai

眼觸所生愛

Craving born of visual contact

śrotrasparśajā tṛṣṇā erh-ch'u-suo-sheng-ai

耳觸所生愛

Craving born of contact with ear

ghrāṇasparśajā tṛṣṇā p'i-ch'u-suo-sheng-ai

鼻觸所生愛

Craving born of contact with nose

jihvāsparśajā tṛṣṇā she-ch'u-suo-sheng-ai

舌觸所生愛

Craving born of contact with tongue

kāyasparśajā tṛṣṇā shen-ch'u-suo-sheng-ai

身觸所生愛

Craving born of contact with body

manaḥsparśajā tṛṣṇā i-ch'u-suo-sheng-ai

意觸所生愛

Craving born of contact with mind

INDEX